RED GREEN'S
BEGINNER'S GUIDE TO
WOMEN

(FOR MEN WHO DON'T READ INSTRUCTIONS)

ALSO BY RED GREEN

How to Do Everything
The Green Red Green

RED GREEN'S
BEGINNER'S GUIDE TO
WOMEN

(FOR MEN WHO DON'T READ INSTRUCTIONS)

Red Green

Doubleday Canada

Doubleday Canada and colophon are registered trademarks of Random House of
Canada Limited

Library and Archives Canada Cataloguing in Publication

Smith, Steve, 1945-, author
    Red Green's beginner's guide to women / Red Green.

Issued in print and electronic formats.
ISBN 978-0-385-67763-9

    1. Man-woman relationships—Humor. 2. Dating
(Social customs)—Humor. I. Title.

PS8587.M589R43 2013   C818'.5402   C2013-902636-3
                                            C2013-903033-6

Cover and text design by Leah Springate
Cover image: Max Smith

Printed and bound in the USA

Published in Canada by Doubleday Canada,
a division of Random House of Canada Limited

www.randomhouse.ca

10 9 8 7 6 5 4 3 2 1

INTRODUCTION

L et me start by congratulating you on having the courage and
maturity to pick up this book. Whether you bought it for
yourself or received it as a gift or borrowed it from a former
friend or are just reading it in a dark corner of a bookstore hoping
you won't be noticed, it shows that you want to be a better
person, which is commendable and possibly essential.

But in the tradition of any of my earlier works, be careful not
to raise your expectations too high. In many ways, difficult
human relationships are like diarrhea—it's important for you to
be the first one to realize you have a problem. And while this
book may not provide a complete cure, it will at least get you
running towards the men's room.

So buying the book is a valuable first step, and the less you
paid, the more valuable it is. Even if you stole the book, you may
have morality issues, but you will probably be the most sensitive
person in your cellblock.

As for the content of the book itself, its purpose is not necessarily to draw conclusions, but more to give observations and
anecdotal evidence that will show the results that come from the
various approaches to the most difficult and yet fundamental of
all human relationships—that of a man and a woman.

And let me make it clear to any of my wife's friends who may
be reading this book that the examples I give here do not in any
way represent my own personal marital experiences. Instead, a
wide array of friends and acquaintances have generously shared

their mistakes so you can avoid them. These people are from all walks of life and many different geographical locations and are even fictitious when necessary. So what you're looking at here is a research book—a collection of experiences and theories that will hopefully help you to understand and cohabitate with your significant other—the most important person in your world—even when she's not in the room.

Red Green

ACKNOWLEDGEMENTS

I want to thank a small collection of Lodge Members who were kind enough to contribute their experiences and opinions and without whose input this book would have been no bigger than a time-share pamphlet. Some might say I have known these men all my life but I say "not yet." And to extend that life as long as possible, I have decided to keep their identities a secret. I will refer to them simply as Buster H., Stinky P., Junior S. and Moose T., as a favour to the Hadfield, Peterson, Singleton and Thompson families respectively.

THE ETERNAL QUESTION

Before we get too far into this thing I think we need to deal with the question of why is it important for us men to understand women. Is it really all that essential, or is it just a cheesy excuse for me to write another book and get a big, fat advance? No, it's not. And it wouldn't have been, even if I did get a big, fat advance.

You are programmed to cohabitate, and unless you're a masochist, you'd like that to be a pleasant lifelong experience. You as a man need to curry favour with at least one woman, and to do that, you have to be able to anticipate her every need and want. And to do *that,* you need to understand her.

So as you go through this frustrating quest to once and for all understand that woman in your life, let's not for one moment forget that if you ever get it right, she will be the greatest thing that ever happened to you. And conversely, if you continue to get it wrong, she will make your life a living hell.

It's a long, arduous route with many pitfalls, but you must always keep your eyes on the prize. And never give up.

MEN ARE FROM MARS, WOMEN ARE FROM MEN

You may remember learning in your Grade 9 biology class that when a man and a woman create a baby, the sex of that baby is determined by the chromosomes of the male sperm, not from those of the female egg. To me that means that the woman was prepared to make either a boy or a girl, depending on what was shipped to her receiving dock.

It's really the first example of a woman's predisposition to make the best of whatever falls into her lap.

That means that, although the two parents share equally in the responsibility for the child's general appearance and personality, the gender of the child comes totally from Dad. So every fertile man in the world has the capability of fathering a female baby, which means that every man in the world should be capable of understanding women, on the basis of local knowledge.

It's probably the origin of the respected phrase "takes one to know one." We have no excuses. It's our first setback.

PUBERTY (IT'S NEVER DONE THAT BEFORE)

I'm not even going to bother with the ages from birth to puberty. Girls are easy to understand during that phase. They're basically boys that you don't ever hit or swear at. Puberty is the game changer. All of a sudden, thirteen years into what has been a pretty good gig, you're suddenly exchanging your high voice for body hair and becoming a deodorant customer and growing like the national debt. Some things that have been hanging around for years suddenly start working. And I'm not talking about your Uncle Bob.

And no matter how tall you are, there seems to be almost no distance between your brain and your genitals. Nor is it always clear who's in charge of who.

This is the beginning of the challenge to be a man. You're having racy thoughts and wild fantasies, and the girls you played hide and seek with last week have no interest in playing hide the cannoli this week. This is where the two genders take different forks in the road. Boys get muscles. Girls get hormones.

And so it begins.

WHAT WOMEN WANT

There is probably no greater mystery facing man since the beginning of time than for him to try to figure out what women want. It's a source of great frustration for men because to them it all seems so simple. They're motivated to give women what they want; they're even prepared to sacrifice if necessary. Many times a man will cry out in the night, "Just tell me what you want," although he's usually alone in the garage at the time.

To find out why this has always been a conundrum, you have to look at the issue from a whole bunch of different sides.

Let's start with the man's perspective. He has a real problem with anybody who can't tell him what they want. If *he* doesn't know what they want, how can he ever provide it? And if *they* don't know what they want, how are they ever going to know when they've got it? Heck, they may already *have* it.

A man is thinking, "How hard can that be?" He knows what *he* wants—fried food, sex, a half-decent house and cool toys. What's the problem? Well, the problem is that men who have those things always want other things, eventually. It's not that they don't want those things at all. It's just that once they get them, the novelty wears off and they move on to something else.

But they continue to know what they want. Men don't see that acquiring bigger boats and more expensive toys and larger portions of fried food is just a repetition of the need to satisfy short-term demands. Every man I know will come up with an instant list of items when you ask him what he wants. But they're all "right now" things. Like winning the lottery or spending a fact-finding half-hour with that blonde at the end of the bar. When you ask them what they want over the long term, for the rest of their lives, the room gets pretty quiet. That's because they don't know what they want, either.

If you ask a woman what she wants "right now," she'll have a lot of quick answers that, with any luck, may include you. But when you just ask her what she wants, she assumes you mean long term, and even if she knows, she doesn't want to answer. Because one of the main things she wants is to not to have to tell you what she wants.

You may be uncomfortable not knowing what she wants, but that's not her problem. Maybe you're uncomfortable with it because you don't really know what *you* want, either, and it kills you to be reminded of that. But don't panic, and don't worry. You don't need to know what your woman wants. You just need to continue to *care* what your woman wants, even if you never find out what it is. The caring will be good enough for her.

Likewise, don't be upset that you don't know what *you* want. Your woman knows what you want and if you play your cards right, she'll make sure you get it. You may not know what it is, but I'm betting you'll recognize it when you see it.

LOVE AT FIRST SITE?

The young people today seem to do everything on the Internet. You ask them what the weather's like right now and they'd rather Google it on their iPhone than look out the window. And when was the last time anybody looked anything up in an encyclopedia? You can look things up on the Internet even if you don't know the alphabet. Every piece of information, every product, every idea, every theory and every*body* is now at your fingertips. Or, more specifically, your thumbtips.

So I guess it's only natural that people would use the Internet to find a partner. You can find your past on the ancestry sites, so maybe you can find your future on the dating sites. And in many ways it's much safer than actual dating. You can stay anonymous as long as you want. You can be thousands of miles away from the other person. And if you do find someone interesting, you can do a background check while you're reading their email.

But I just want you to be careful about what you're doing. You could be playing with virtual fire. I think some of the appeal of Internet dating is that people think it's another innovation in the recent string of computer technological breakthroughs. And sometimes when something is new, people will be drawn to it for its newness rather than its value.

Maybe the technology of being able to send instant messages and videos to people all over the world is new, but the concept of getting romantically involved with someone you've never met goes back to biblical times. Back in those days it was called "arranged marriages," and maybe the principals weren't involved, but if you let your dad use your laptop, history may repeat itself.

In more recent centuries we've had mail-order brides, where some lonely guy who'd been rejected by everyone in his own country would write a letter to a woman in the Far East who was looking to relocate to the Far West, and if she was agreeable, he would FedEx her to the nearest port of entry. Sure it took longer because of the letters going back and forth, but that gave each of them more time to reconsider.

But think about this: you're each on a path that will lead you to a person who has been passed over by every person they, and their mother, have ever met. The Internet is quicker, but that doesn't mean it's better. And even with all the information available, you still know less about the person than you don't know about the person.

You may think they have language skills from their emails, but they could be using spell check and auto-grammar. They may send a picture so you know what they look like, but even I can go through a thousand pictures of myself and find one that looks okay. Even though it doesn't look like me. Which is why it looks okay. Even a short video of them can be deceiving. You give him a couple of thousand takes and even Sly Stallone comes off as an actor.

What you get on the Internet is a very produced, edited, air-brushed, polished version of the person. You're not seeing the real thing. You're not going to know if she has hairy hands or eats with her mouth open. Don't get fooled by the brochure. You want to do a little test drive before you sign on the dotted line.

I'm not saying the Internet is a bad way to meet women. I'm just saying you should lower your expectations or you're going to be disappointed. A friend of mine who tried it said he heard back from hundreds of women and his conclusion was "the odds are good but the goods are odd."

GETTING HER ATTENTION

With any luck, you will know early on if you are heterosexual. Once that's established, you will want to begin your quest to find a lifemate or, failing that, a weekend shack-up. In either case, no woman of the opposite sex is going to be attracted to you until she at least *notices* you. You have to get her attention. And that can be a tough challenge.

Stinky P. told me about the first girl he tried to impress. She had a backyard pool, so Stinky ran into the yard next door and screamed "Geronimo!" as he vaulted over the fence and did a fully extended bellyflop into her swimming pool. Unfortunately, he assumed she'd be home and watching. He also assumed there'd be water in the pool.

Moose T. had a party trick that all the guys liked, so he tried that to get noticed. He would eat a hearty meal of pickled vegetables and carbonated beverages and, after about an hour of abdominal exercises and resource management, was able to pass wind in a way that allowed him to perform the entire Canadian national anthem, including one verse in French.

But however you plan to get a girl's attention, make sure you focus on her reaction to see how it's going. If Moose had only noticed the look of shock and disgust on the girl's face, he could have cut the performance right after "our home and native land," but instead he just kept blasting away with his eyes closed until the concert was violently terminated by someone trying to light a scented candle. But that's the kind of thing you do when you're thirteen. And when you're Moose.

What both of these guys failed to realize is that they had reached the point in their lives when they were looking at what society calls "negative options." That's because their reference level was a bunch of other guys like themselves. There was nobody in that group that could give them the slightest hint of what these girls would find interesting or amusing. The sad truth is that what most thirteen-year-old boys find entertaining, most thirteen-year-old girls find repulsive.

So instead of trying to impress girls with what you say or what you do, which we all know is a long shot at best, I suggest you appeal to their mercy. You can claim to be having trouble with a certain school subject and ask them to help you with your homework. You may think you'll have to pretend you're stupid, but it may not be necessary.

Another surefire way to get a girl's attention is to hurt yourself badly in front of her and then act like you're fine. Coming down a flight of cement stairs while straddling the crossbar of your bike oughta do it. Her natural nursing instincts will kick in and you will have her undivided attention at least until you regain consciousness.

GROOM FOR IMPROVEMENT

If you're a reasonable-looking teenaged boy who does okay at school and has a few friends and has never done hard time at juvie, and yet has had no luck in attracting a girlfriend, the problem could be your grooming. It's a sad fact that, on average, girls are much more particular than us about the level of grooming—i.e., refinement—of anyone who expresses an interest in them.

And to make matters worse, girls notice things. Things that you and your friends would ignore, they can't. Or won't. But mainly don't.

Now, I know you were hoping that some good-looking unattached girl would find you acceptable, but unfortunately, Fantasyland is at Disney World. You have to live in the real world. So if you've been striking out on a regular basis, you may be surprised by these examples of the level of grooming and personal hygiene that girls demand:

- You can't wear the same clothes today that you wore yesterday, even if they smell sort of okay.
- If a piece of cheese has mould on it or teeth marks from a mouse, you have to throw the whole thing away rather than just hack off the bad part.
- It's not okay to have a stain on your clothes, even if it's dry.
- If you only do the laundry once a week, you need seven pairs of underwear.
- Your hair should be clean enough that people can see the individual strands.
- You may have heard that girls are attracted by the smell of pheromones in a boy's sweat, but it's better if you never meet those girls.
- Torn jeans are only cool if the holes are in the right places.

- Your fingernails shouldn't look like you just gave a paved road a backscratch.
- Every person should have exactly two eyebrows. No more, no less.
- Teeth need to be white and should never be seen in groups of fewer than twelve.
- Buy a full-length mirror and don't be afraid to use it.

A LITTLE GENTILITY

To be fair to us guys, a lot of us are victims of our own upbringing. Generally, there's a lot more time and energy put into the raising of a daughter than a son. I'm not sure why that is. Maybe there's a sense that a boy will find some way to survive no matter what; maybe it dates back to the time when the goal was to get your daughter married off; maybe parents just don't like sons as much as daughters. But whatever the reason, a young man often goes out into the world without being fully prepared.

He may have a basic grasp of a reliable work ethic and he may generally treat people in a decent and fair way. But in the area of social graces, he may be totally ignorant. That's because nobody ever taught him about such things. Whatever he knows he got from watching his dad, and that's rarely a good thing.

Okay, maybe a million years ago, social grace was not an essential skill. A man's main purpose was to provide food, shelter and protection for his wife and family, and the better he did that, the better a catch he was. Well, things have changed. If you want to attract a woman today, you'd better have some gentility. It doesn't make you less of a man to be polite and even chivalrous. Quite the opposite. Many women these days are looking for a man to not only be strong and intelligent, but also refined. It's really just the next step in our evolution.

And from what I've seen, a lot of us are being left behind. I know men who will openly scratch themselves in public. They'll scratch their stomach or their back or their *lower* back or worse. I've seen them rub themselves up against brick buildings like a bear on a day trip. You don't see women doing that. I've seen men spit on the sidewalk and relieve themselves at the side of the road. Men who should say, "Please excuse me for a moment, dear," will instead say, "I'm gonna go take a dump."

Come on, we need to evolve a little here. We're supposed to be at the absolute top of the animal chain and yet man is the only species who picks his nose. I don't think that's what Darwin had in mind. And picking your nose while driving your car doesn't make it somehow okay. Why is it always men doing that? Do you know how tough that makes it for the rest of us? Women think we're all the same, so when they see one guy doing something disgusting, they think we're all capable of it. And they're right. So stop doing that. Or at least stop doing it outdoors or anywhere where there are other people and a light source. Let's see a little refinement, a little gentility. What kind of a woman do you hope to attract when you're standing there scratching your crotch with one hand while picking your nose with the other?

It's like hitchhiking with a chainsaw. The normal people are not going to stop to give you a ride. And when somebody does stop, you have to ask yourself, "What kind of a person would pick up a guy carrying a chainsaw?"

CHEST FEVER

The attraction of the female bosom is a strange phenomenon that affects almost all men. It's hard to explain. Maybe it's the fascination of seeing something you can never have. Maybe it's the envy of a woman having a body part that combines form and function.

Whatever the reason, men have been interested in breasts since the beginning of time. They give them nicknames—boobs, bazooms, bazookas, cans, honkers, hoops, jugs, rack, ta-tas, the Twins, the Giants, and the Forty-Niners. There's even a restaurant chain named after them. The attraction of breasts is a tremendous disadvantage to men. They have to constantly fight their desire to see them and touch them and who knows what all. Some men can have an entire conversation with a busty woman without ever making eye contact. A woman wearing a 44D halter top ran into a bar and stole a handful of cash and, when the police arrived, not one guy could describe her face.

We've come a long way in the last fifty years regarding our attitudes towards equality of opportunity for women—equal pay for equal work, the removal of the glass ceiling, Oprah, etc. But because of men's obsession with the female form, we have to stay vigilant. And the women need to admit they're part of the problem. While nobody wants to be ogled, a woman will rightfully use whatever assets she has, to attract a man, be chosen for a job, or basically get whatever she wants.

Nobody in the advertising business is disgusted with men's attraction to a healthy bosom. When they put a couple of bikini-clad models in front of a minivan, it looks like a Ferrari. I know they say sex sells, but to me this attraction is not even sexual. It's more like being awestruck by a unique example of kinetic art that is simultaneously soft and firm, that changes with movement but then reverts back to its original shape, and is part of a living being. Men find that ~~titillating~~ fascinating.

What makes it even more indefinable is that for most men, there is an ideal range of breast size. As teenagers, they think the bigger the better, but as an adult in the real world, there is a point where the body proportions are so out of whack that the beauty is lost. I would say most men prefer breasts to be in the upper range of normal. And so do women. Many will have breast implants or reductions to get themselves into that range. (Most women don't bother. They just use their intellect and personality to get through life, which we all know is the best way to go, but it's not what I'm talking about right now.)

So let's all admit that we have a problem here. The whole mammary obsession thing objectifies women and impairs men. A man's IQ drops 10 per cent with every one-inch increase in a woman's bust size. The woman who shows the greatest amount of cleavage will have the most conversations and the least eye contact. So, is the answer to force women to wear clothing that goes right up to the neck? I hope not.

I think the best solution is for us all to be aware of the issue but to act like it doesn't exist. Kind of like the government does with almost everything. Whenever you're speaking to a woman with large breasts, make intelligent conversation and look into her face. If she's selling something, get your wife in on the decision. (Unless she *is* your wife, in which case, you can't lose.)

And men everywhere: do not ever make any reference to the size of the woman's chest. She knows she's got it and she knows you like it, but as soon as you point it out, it ruins it for all men everywhere. Being a gentleman means taking one for the team. Or in this case, taking two for the team.

SEXIST TEST

If you want to be a fully evolved human male, you have to eventually grow out of your immature tendencies to see women as sex objects. You're not going to have successful relationships with women until you can see them as bright, competent, complex individuals who have the right to all of life's opportunities without prejudice.

This test is a way for you to see how you're doing in that area. For each of the women listed, choose the answer that most represents what came to your mind first when you read her name.

Dolly Parton
   a) singer
   b) songwriter
   c) actress
   d) other

Monica Lewinsky
   a) political aide
   b) media personality
   c) college graduate
   d) other

Heidi Fleiss
   a) entrepreneur
   b) Hollywood socialite
   c) matchmaker
   d) other

Lady Godiva
   a) political activist
   b) horsewoman
   c) victim of global warming
   d) other

Scoring: Award yourself 50 points for every time you answered a), 40 points for b), 30 points for c), and no points for d). Now total them up.

What Your Score Means

150–200 - - - - - - - - - - - - - -	Enlightened Male
100–150 - - - - - - - - - - - - - -	Better than Most
50–100 - - - - - - - - - - - - - -	Most
0–50 - - - - - - - - - - - - - - -	Counselling Needed

SURPRISE SURPRISE

When you become a mature, single adult—or, failing that, a single adult—you need to get yourself one of those fancy cellphones that does everything from identifying constellations to reading your alcohol level. There's a pretty good chance this phone will have the ability to make audio recordings. It will even be able to do *secret* audio recording while it's tucked away in your pocket. But the microphone is sensitive, so it's very important which of your pockets you put it in, and please don't ask why. But once you've established a pocket that's far away from any unfortunate ambient noise, you want to start making secret recordings at certain kinds of events.

I'm talking about events where there is a potential for you to be surprised about something. That's the whole point of the exercise—to get recordings of you being honestly surprised. So start recording when it's your birthday or when the boss has asked you to come to his office or when you're talking to your doctor or your accountant.

Hopefully, in a short period of time you will have a selection of recordings of you being honestly surprised. You need to study these to learn every nuance and expression. Every detail of tempo and timing. What, specifically, do you say when you're surprised? And at what volume? Is it a short, loud burst of energy or is it a lot of repetitious statements expressed at a medium volume over an extended period? It is absolutely essential that you not only become infinitely aware of your surprise response but that you also teach yourself how to mimic that response so well that it will defy detection. That's because when the day comes when you find yourself married and wanting to stay that way, there is no more important talent than the ability to successfully fake surprise.

That's due to the unfortunate fact of life that wives are not dumb. They know you better than you know yourself. And yet they married you, so go figure. One of the reasons they know us so well is because they pay close attention to our patterns. They know the kinds of things we do and think and say. They also know that we like to avoid problems whenever possible. And one of the ways we do that is by not being completely open and honest about things we've said or done that haven't gone exactly the way we planned. We often revert back to being an eight-year-old boy in school trying to blame the puddle under his chair on someone else.

Wives know we do that, and it makes them sneaky. If they come home and see the barbecue is missing a lid, they won't just come into the house and ask, "What did you do to the barbecue?" That's way too easy for us. Instead they'll ask, "So how was your day?" And they'll pretend to be offhand. They may not even look at you or stop walking while you answer, but their ears are on maximum alert for anything that just doesn't sound right. For example, you. Now, obviously, "How was your day?" is not going to hurt you, but it's not supposed to. It's the set-up question. It's like "Please tell the court your name." The tough questions are coming next. Like "What happened to the barbecue?" Not too bad, but we've obviously gone to the next level. Keep your answer simple. The more you say, the deeper you go—"You mean somebody blew the lid off it? Or something?" Don't do that. Just say, "How do you mean?" Now she'll walk right up to you, stare you in the eye and say, "The lid's gone."

This is where all the training and rehearsal pays off. You will be surprised in such a totally convincing way that she will drop the line of questioning and never get to the part about the blow-torch or the aviation-fuel charcoal starter. You will live to barbecue another day. There's another surprise.

BREAKING THE ICE

I know this is uncomfortable for any teenaged boy to hear, but once you get a girl's attention, to move the relationship forward you are going to have to speak to her at some point.

It's always easier to do when there's an obvious need for you to communicate—like when she's asking you what time it is or wondering why you're sitting on her bike. But sometimes you just have to be able to strike up a conversation based on nothing.

This is not a natural behavioural trait for men. Those with the knack often have many girlfriends and wives simultaneously. They also make excellent time-share salesmen. However, if you're one of the vast majority that finds it hard to talk to strangers—and even harder to *want* to talk to strangers, this can be a challenge.

The following is a passage from Buster's Diary which he said I could quote—or I'm sure he would have done if he'd known I had the diary. Buster was fourteen when he made this entry:

Dear Diary,

I was hanging around the school after class, waiting for Ann to come out so I could get a chance to introduce myself and maybe even walk her home and then kiss her on her front porch or anywhere she'd let me. But failing that I would at least say hello to her. When she finally came out she was with three other girls. The other three saw me and immediately went back inside. Ann didn't and continued on her way. I thought this was an excellent sign. I went right up to her and said hi. She didn't answer but she looked at me. SHE LOOKED AT ME. How cool is that? It wasn't exactly a friendly look. Women are so mysterious. Then I said, "Which way are you going?" She pointed down Queen St. I said, "Wow! So am I!" She said, "Really?" SHE SPOKE TO ME. SHE ACTUALLY SPOKE TO ME. HOLY CRAP! Then she yawned and walked away. I followed her. "Is it okay if I walk with you?" I asked. "No," she said and yawned again. That's twice she's spoken to me. This is now officially a conversation. "Well, I'll just stay back here then," I said. I kept about ten feet behind her but yelled so she could still hear me. I had lots of questions. "Who's your favourite wrestler?" "Would you like a pierogi?" "Do you want to stop at Moose's house and hear him play the anthem?" No response. But it was fun sort of walking with her. She even looked as good from the back as she did from the front. Kind of like a Studebaker. She was in good shape. Very fit. But then she runs a lot. At least she did that day. And she was really moving. I kept up as best I could but I know she must have been exhausted by the time she reached her house and that's why she went in and slammed the door without saying goodbye. I hung around her place for a few hours thinking about what a great day this had been, but I went home right after the police told me to.

I know many of you find it difficult to break the ice with women, and there are a large number of men who don't like to talk to anybody about anything, but talking to an attractive woman is a skill you'll want to master. I don't have a lot of positive advice in that area, but from personal experience, I suggest you keep the conversation light and breezy. Try to focus on topics that interest her and let her do most of the talking.

As a starting point, here is a list of subjects to avoid:

- flu symptoms
- nuclear fission
- cannibalism
- rite-of-passage tribal rituals
- phlegm
- waste disposal
- erectile dysfunction

THE PHOTO GALLERY

For those of you who need visual reinforcement to be able to understand a concept, I thought it might be helpful to use an imaginary photo gallery to demonstrate some of the basic differences between men and women. If they each had their own photo gallery, here are examples of some of the things that would be on display:

HERS

HIS

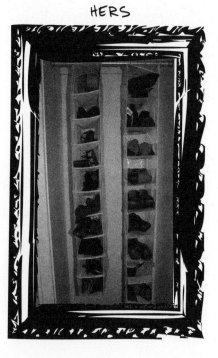

HERS   HIS

 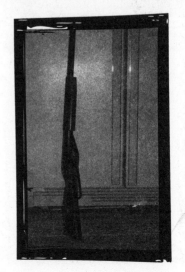

HERS HIS

 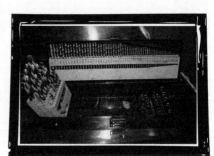

HERS   HIS

THE PARTY POLICY

Once you've broken the ice, the next challenge is to get yourself into social situations where the girl in question is going to be. It would be nice if you were already in her social circle and being invited to the same parties, but if you're a fan of mine and also reading this book, that's probably not the case. So you need to create a social event where the two of you will be allowed to advance your relationship in a way that may eventually lead to dating, then intimacy, followed by three or four children and, perhaps one day, marriage.

But you need to start with what I like to call a "party." It can be as formal as bowling or as casual as prying coins out of parking meters. Some call it a party, others call it gang violence, but let's not get bogged down in semantics. The point is to get a bunch of young people of similar interests doing something together that somehow makes you look more acceptable to the girl who is the object of your affection.

Now, you could take your chances and wait until a friend has a party and invites the two of you to be there, but I don't recommend it. You need to control the variables or you're dead. There are probably a lot of better-looking, available, nicer guys in your town, and if even one of them shows up, you're toast.

So you need to be in charge of the guest list. The A-list should be made up of good-looking, well-liked teenaged couples from your peer group. They will create a feeling of beauty and happiness that you could never pull off on your own, and the fact that they are all couples will send a subtle message to you-know-who that the two of you really need to hook up. To round out the guest roster, go to the B-list, which should consist of total losers. They will be easy to find because they're probably already your best friends and they are always available. Just be sure to avoid inviting anyone who is available and a better catch than you. Let them have their own parties.

Now that you have the guest list, you need to pick the right location. Try to avoid having the party at your house, because there's a lot of potential for embarrassment in your own home. Whether it's your extra-absorbent underwear hanging on the line or your retainer swinging from the fridge door or the parole officer dropping by to check on your stepdad, there are just too many things that can go wrong. I recommend a friend's home or somebody's home or a model home—lots of them available since the real-estate crash. The main criteria is that you want a house with a basement. The earth is an excellent planet for deadening noise, the spilled drinks have nowhere to go, and nobody ever falls out of basement windows. Once you have the venue, you need to pick the menu. Don't choose anything that needs to be hot or cold, since the power is probably off.

I don't think you can go wrong with Honey Nut Cheerios. They're filling, they're healthy, they're a natural source of something or other, and as primarily a breakfast cereal, they imply to the special guest that if she'd like to have a sleepover, you've got it covered.

I'm assuming your guests are all too young to drink alcohol, so I recommend American beer. Now we come to the most important aspect of your party: the activities. Here are some great party games that will jumpstart your budding relationship:

The Eskimo Game

The boy and girl stand facing each other with their hands behind their backs and wearing white T-shirts. Unwrap a melting Eskimo Pie and put one end into each of their mouths. The challenge is for each of them to eat their half before the chocolate drips on their shirts. The reason it's called the Eskimo Game is because you also place a dollop of Krazy Glue on the tip of each of their noses so if they accidentally kiss Eskimo-style, it will be a case of endless love.

Pass the Fruit

The boys and girls line up against opposite walls, facing each other. Each of them is given a selection of fruit. The boys start by holding an orange under their chin using only their neck muscles. They have to carry it like that all the way to the girls' line and transfer the orange to their partner's neck without using their hands. Don't be confused by the term "navel orange"—you need to keep it up in the neck region. (If any of the guests has a goitre, you can allow them to use a tangerine instead.) For the next round, the girls put a zucchini under each armpit and must transfer it to the boys' armpits, again without using their hands. For the final exchange, the boys must carry a fifteen-pound watermelon between their thighs across the room and transfer it to the girls. Be sure to alert them that if they fail to pass the watermelon test, they "cantaloupe." Everybody loves that kind of laugh-out-loud humour.

Where Have Those Lips Been?

For this game you'll need to bring some glass microscope slides home from biology class. Don't steal them, but it's fine to borrow them forever. Get the boys to leave the room while the girls smear on a ton of lipstick and then each one kisses a different slide. Now the boys return and, one by one, take turns being the screen for a slide show in which a slide of a girl's lips is projected on the boy's body somewhere and the rest of the guests have to guess whose lips they are and what are they doing there.

I'd Like to See More of You

In this game, somebody turns out the lights and the girls all take off their blouses. (I may have those steps reversed.) The boys are handcuffed behind their backs, which many of them may be used to. Now the whole crowd just mingles in the dark. There are only two rules—no talking and the boys are not allowed to walk backwards. Each time a boy bumps into someone, he has to guess who it is. If he guesses one of the other boys, he is disqualified. In order to speed up the game, the host, at his discretion, may flick on the lights for a moment or two. Whoever identifies the most girls correctly gets their own reality show. (I'm not sure this is an actual game. I may have dreamt it.)

We're a Couple Now (The Railroad Game)

You'll need a coat hanger for each person for this game. The boys mount their coat hangers horizontally through their belt loops in the front of their pants. The girls mount their coat hangers vertically on their lower back. Each boy is given an electronic bicycle horn to sound and a list of simple instructions:

One short beep - - - - - - - - - - - Turn left
Two short beeps - - - - - - - - - - Turn right
One long beep - - - - - - - - - - - Back up
One medium beep - - - - - - - - - Go forward
One really loud and long beep - - - Stop

The girls are blindfolded and lined up in front of their boyfriends, with their backs to them. When the game starts, the girls back up towards the boys as if they're train engines trying to hook up to the caboose. The boys cannot talk to them but can only use their horns to communicate. The first couple to engage the coat hangers and successfully pull out of the station is the winner. But the main focus of fun is the chaos of six or seven of these loud horns giving simultaneous signals. Talk about a laugh riot!

Perhaps you'd rather play different games, and I say fine . . . whatever . . . I couldn't care less. But I would advise that you limit your vulnerability by making each game somebody else's idea, and don't be afraid to glare at them if anything goes wrong. It also might be good to have a public defender on speed dial. Even if the party is a complete disaster, it will lead to further conversation because you will need to apologize to that special girl. This will be a recurring pattern throughout the relationship.

PRIMARY ASSESSMENT

In all personal dealings with women, from the most distant to the most intimate, you should never get ahead of yourself. The best way to protect against that is to make regular assessments to ensure you fully understand the current status of your relationship.

This is one of those times. You've introduced yourself, you've been in group situations, both formal and casual, and before you get too focused on taking the next step, you need to clearly identify your current position. To do that, you'll need to use your friends. Don't feel bad, that's what they're for.

The first request is to have your friends ask around about the girl to see if she has any boyfriends on the horizon and, more specifically, if one of them is you. Next, you need one of your friends to walk down the school corridor about ten feet behind you. As you pass the girl standing with her friends, wave to her. Just a casual friendly wave, not a jumping-up-and-down-flailing-both-arms-in-the-air-with-a-"pick-me"-look-on-your-face kind of wave. After the wave, avert your eyes and walk by. Now your friend has to intently watch her reaction. If she turns to her friends, smiles and blushes a little, and says, "That's the guy," that's good. If she rolls her eyes and says, "That's the guy," that's a whole different message. If she jerks her head away and mimes vomiting, that doesn't mean you should completely give up hope, but almost.

The worst reaction your friend could report is no reaction at all—she doesn't change her facial expression or body language and doesn't even recognize your existence. That's the real killer. You have a lot more chance with a girl who doesn't like you than with a girl who doesn't acknowledge you. Going forward, your actions should be based on the knowledge you just acquired. If you got a positive reaction, keep doing what you're doing. The more negative reaction, the more things you need to change. But there is a limit. If you have to change your personality, looks, weight, height and gender, it's probably time to move on. If you think you're doing okay or you think there's a chance that you're okay, the only way you're going to find out for sure is to ask her out on a date.

THE FIRST DATE

From Buster's diary:

Dear Diary,

Just got home from my first date. It's 9:30. Did not go well. Apparently "smart casual" does not include bib overalls. We had nothing in common. She didn't even laugh at my goat joke. When I stopped the car on Lovers' Lane, she got out and walked home. My life is over. Thinking about moving to Sudbury.

I'm going to skip over the first few years because a date isn't a date until you're old enough to drive your own vehicle. Having your mom drive you, or picking the girl up on your bike or your skateboard, is just lame. Now, maybe some of you live on a farm in one of those areas where you're allowed to drive farm vehicles at the age of twelve, but I think you should wait until you have a proper licence, because bad things can happen when you take a combine to a drive-in movie.

So let's assume you're sixteen and have a valid driver's licence. You are now ready to ask that special girl out on your first date. This is a big step that may involve rejection, and by far the most important aspect of it is for you to retain enough of your own pride and self-respect to be able to live a relatively normal life. So the first thing you need to do is to assume that she's going to say no. And when she does, you're going to need something to blame it on that has nothing to do with you.

Maybe you picked the wrong date, or maybe she's not feeling well or maybe she doesn't enjoy monster trucks. Whatever it is, you have to build those safety valves into your presentation when you ask for the date. Don't ever ask, "Would you like to go out with me sometime?" Suppose she bursts out laughing or says, "Really?"— not in a good way—or yells some insensitive message that's painfully clear and loud enough for everyone to hear. What then?

You did a dumb thing. You didn't specify a date or an activity or anything. What you presented was the two of you doing something together, sometime, somewhere. You were basically saying you are available 24/7 to go anywhere with her and do anything she wants. It was an offer with only one condition: you. And she declined. There's no coming back from that. You're going to end up in the French Foreign Legion or the clergy. You've got to protect yourself from that. You've got to protect the clergy from that.

So pick a specific date and a specific activity. And do some research. Find out what the cool couples are doing over the next few weeks. Maybe there's some big rap artist coming to town who wears his hat sideways and his pants around his ankles to distract you from his lack of talent. Get yourself a couple of tickets and a licence to carry a concealed weapon and you're good to go.

Now you've really improved your bargaining position on the date front. You're asking her to go somewhere that kids she admires are already going, and you've already bought the tickets, which tells her you'll be going there with somebody else if she says no. (Do not mention your sister.) So here's how you ask, "Hey, the gang is all going to the PP Diddly Squat concert and I've got a couple of front-row tickets. I got a list of people I'd like to take, but you're the first one on it. Lemme know if you wanna go."

You have now almost completely depersonalized the invitation, which is the key to successful dating. All she hears is the "great tickets" to a concert the "right people" are already going to. You're the smallest thing in the equation. It not only makes it unlikely that she'll say no, it allows you to rationalize the rejection as her turning her back on all of her friends and PP—and from what I hear, this is not a guy you should ever turn your back on.

Chances are she'll say yes, but even if she doesn't, you're covered. And your sister will owe you huge.

What to Wear

I know you're completely unprepared for this question because up until now you either didn't care, your mother was dressing you, or both. But suddenly what you're wearing is crucial.

As Buster discovered, your appearance is never neutral. It sends either a negative or a positive signal about you, how you feel about yourself and how you feel about the girl you're taking out—and, most important, how you feel about the parents of the girl you're taking out. Because when you ring that doorbell there will be two very skeptical adults doing a full-body scan on you. They don't want to see ripped jeans or multiple body piercings or a drawing of cartoon animals mating on your T-shirt. But you can't go overboard on the nerdy end, either, with cargo pants or a fedora or a bow tie.

You want to go with conservative cool. Don't dress like a rock star, dress like one of the backup singers. And don't try to look rich, especially if you're not. Looking poor looks way richer than trying to look rich. I know this is hard for you because I'm asking you to pretend you care about something that you don't, but if you can't do that, this relationship is going nowhere.

The Wheels

Even more important than what you wear is what you drive. Long before you arrive, her parents are secretly peeking out the window to see what kind of vehicle they are being asked to let their daughter leave in. They don't want to see a 1981 Dodge Aries with rust issues and a cloud of blue smoke pouring out of the exhaust, even if you park it so the bullet holes are on the far side.

Don't let your pride get in the way. They'd much rather see you pull up in a $20,000 car you borrowed than in an $800 car you own. Go with your best option. Maybe your mom's car would be comforting to other parents. Or borrow your dad's company car, unless he drives a hearse or an Oscar Mayer Wienermobile.

And make sure her father knows that you know that he noticed the car you're driving. The girl's mother is hoping you're a nice boy; her father doesn't believe nice boys exist, so he'll settle for a nice car.

Getting There

Let's say, for argument's sake, that her parents couldn't come up with a good enough reason to call off the date and you've just left her house and are walking towards your car. *You are not safe yet.* Her parents are squished in behind the side curtain panels and watching your every move. Don't reach out to hold the girl's hand. If you accidentally miss and touch some other part of her, there's not an excuse in the world that her father would accept— as he comes screaming out of the house brandishing a 12-gauge.

Just walk at a comfortable pace and comment on the weather or something neutral like that. She's not interested in hearing about your shower or what you had for dinner. Open the passenger door for her and make sure she gets in. All of her. Slamming the door on her foot is not a good way to start a date.

Make sure she puts on her seatbelt. If she's having trouble with it, don't help her. Dad's still at the window and he's got the safety off. Drive away slowly. Let her wave to her parents if she wants to. You need to avoid hitting trees, fire hydrants and somebody's dog—especially *her* dog.

Don't try to make conversation; you're nervous and you'll just say something stupid. Let her do the talking. If she doesn't talk, turn on the radio. If the radio doesn't work, this date is pretty much over. If the radio does work, don't sing along with the songs or talk along with the commercials. It's far too early in the relationship for her to see how annoying you can be.

The main focus of whatever you say and do should be her. Think about how she's going to react before you blurt something out. Junior S. tells me about a mistake he made on his first date. His uncle was a fisherman who used to carry his pills around in a prophylactic to keep them dry. He asked Junior to pick him up a box of them. On the way to the movies they were going right by the drugstore, so Junior pulled over and said to his date, "I'm just going in here to get some condoms." When he returned, she was gone. You've got to anticipate her point of view so you'll be able to avoid problems. Later in your life you'll realize that's impossible, but it's still important to try.

Being There

After you arrive and park, you may notice as you're walking through the parking lot that your date is scanning the crowd, looking for her friends. This is why it's so important that you hang on to both of your tickets. Even though you want to be wanted, the truth is you need to be needed.

Once inside, go directly to your seats. This is why you bought great seats. Her friends may be cool, but they're cheap, so they won't be sitting anywhere near you. Also, you want to be sitting there when they arrive so they can see you're with her and that you obviously have unlimited disposable income. Once the concert starts, do whatever she does. If she just sits there, you just sit there. If she gets up and dances, you get up and dance. If she throws her bra at the stage, you go up and get it back.

It's important that she feels like she's in charge and that you approve of whatever she does. That's the best way to get a second date.

At the intermission, offer to go and get her something to eat or drink. If she wants a drink, that's easy, but if she wants something to eat, you have to think about this. You can't let her eat alone, so you'll have to have something too. What you choose will determine your romantic future.

First of all, there's nothing that you're allowed to eat with your mouth open, so abandon that dream. The best choice is to have exactly what she's having, but maybe you don't care for hummus. Even so, don't choose anything that has a stronger flavour than what she's having. Don't ever be the only one eating garlic. If you have gaps between your teeth, you have to be extra careful with your food choice. Small chunks of ground beef or black licorice will wedge between your teeth and make your smile look like a piano. And it's hard to look cool while flossing. So either order something that's almost a liquid or buy a tooth-coloured sandwich.

If she declines food or drink, keep encouraging her to change her mind. It's good for you to send a subtle message that you're attentive and an excellent provider.

In the second half of the concert, you'll probably both be sitting down. If the conversation is going well and she seems to like you, or at least be able to tolerate you, you can test the waters by slowly sliding your arm over the top of her seat—the one she's sitting on top of, not the one she's sitting on. Don't make contact until you're both aware that your arm is there. Then you can slowly and gently make contact with her shoulders and watch her reaction. If she pulls away, apologize and pretend you extended your arm so you could see your watch. (Make sure to wear a watch.)

If she doesn't react at all, you're in great shape, with one small warning: YOU CANNOT, FOR ANY REASON WHATSO-EVER, RETRACT THAT ARM FOR THE REST OF THE CONCERT. It might go numb and turn purple, but you can't take it back without sending a horrible message. You need to think about that before you stick your arm out there in the first place. In the weeks before the date, you should see how long you can ride your bike while signalling for a right-hand turn.

You should also Google the act's previous concerts to see how long the show is going to be. You're better to err on the side of caution. You might think you have it timed right, but a fifteen-minute encore can lead to gangrene.

Driving Her Home

By far the most important part of the date is the drive home. The period of nervous evaluation is over. You're finished with the interview and oral exam, and now it's time for the results.

But you can't just say, "Well, how do you like me now?" Not unless you're a masochist or Toby Keith. You have to sense it in her body language. Especially if her body language is French. If she leans against you while you're walking to the car, or if she brushes by you as you hold the car door for her and then waits for you to close it, and then open it again so she can free her scarf, these are good signs.

It's in the way she talks to you. If she seems animated and happy, she may have enjoyed herself, or maybe she's just excited about being able to go home. If she's talking about other couples or personal things, that's good. If she talks about non-personal things like mononucleosis, the good-night kiss is a longshot.

If you have any hope of sustaining a long-term relationship with a woman, you have to accept that the past and the future are mean-ingless—it's how she feels about you right now that matters. So just because the date has gone well to this point means nothing.

You can't rest on your laurels. You don't have any laurels, and if you want to be with a woman, you can't rest on anything.

So keep it light and perky all the way home. If you're brave enough, you could subtly mention some other event happening at some point in the future but you're not sure if you'll be available to go. You're fishing and she knows it, but that's okay. You're at least letting her know that you're open to a second date if your busy schedule will allow. On the one hand it's not easy to put yourself on the line like that, but on the other hand you have to or you're just wasting time. If she's not interested in you, it's better for you to find out now rather than after you've booked the church and named all the children.

Walk her to the door, but don't try any funny stuff. Not even any mildly amusing stuff. Just thank her and say goodnight and for God's sake don't cry.

Après-Date Follow-Up

The first date is one of those things in life where you really don't know how it went until long after it's done. Kind of like making a baby.

Unless you want to pretend nothing ever happened, the best approach is to wait a week or two and then give her a call and see what's what. If she answers the phone, that's a good sign because chances are she has caller ID. Tell her how much fun the date had been. Give her a short beat to agree, and if she doesn't, press on. If she interrupts you with a list of bad things that happened on the date, claim amnesia or temporary insanity—or permanent insanity.

She's expecting you to ask her out on another date, but don't do it. It's better to keep her guessing a little, even though you're just pretending her guesses are wrong. Ask her for help of some kind, like doing a charity car wash (just your car) or helping you out with a book report that was due five months ago. It'll take the pressure of a date out of the equation and you can't lose. If she already finds you interesting, this will just enhance that feeling, and if she doesn't, this is the kind of curveball that can make her forget she doesn't like you. The working-together thing may be just the ticket for her to get used to your idiosyncracies, and in many cases it sets her up to accept that all-important second date. Even if it's just out of curiosity.

If she accepts your invitation, please proceed to the next section of this book. If she doesn't, please go back to Getting Her Attention and repeat all of the steps with a different girl until you're allowed to go to the next level. If you run out of girls that you know, you will either have to transfer to a larger school or win the lottery.

RAMPING UP

As you work your way through the next series of dates, you will have your ups and downs, your fights and your happy moments. It's all part of the dance as you cautiously reveal, intentionally or not, your true character.

Don't be over-sensitive about her difficulty accepting every little nuance of your behaviour. I know the guys think you're great, but none of them is prepared to marry you and have your children. They don't really think you're great; you're just great enough for the things you do with them—fishing or hunting or playing mailbox baseball. You may have one guy who calls himself your best buddy, but as soon as you put your arm around him and start slow dancing, watch the change in attitude. Even your mom doesn't like everything about you, so don't expect your girlfriend to.

But other than those little speed bumps, you'll probably find that things are progressing just fine until the sixth or seventh date. By that time the word is out and it's affecting your lives.

Other boys know you're dating her and have stopped calling. Other girls know she's dating you and are curiously baffled. It's time for you to either break up with this girl (what, are you crazy?) or you need to make a commitment (what, are you crazy?!) because your relationship is like a hand of poker: you've both anted, she placed a bet, you called, got no answer but called back, and now it's time to see another card.

The only way to do that is to ask her to "go steady"—to date only you as a trial, to see if you really are prepared to spend your lives together—or at least a dirty weekend, but you'll only mention the "lives together" part. And like a good poker player, she'll suspect you're bluffing. She'll be looking for the "tells"—the signs that you're not as sincere as the guy she wants to be with needs to be.

But don't do it lightly. Once you place that bet and she calls, you're going to have to play the hand all the way to the end. And you may have to go "all in."

YOU AND ETHYL

Alcohol has played a role in the relationship between men and women for thousands of years. It's often used to finalize a marriage or to initiate a conception.

There's an old Latin expression, *"In vino veritas,"* which means "That's wine, for sure," and the inference is the more you drink, the more honest you get. I have yet to meet a drunk who confirms that theory. There are some other misconceptions about drinking that you'll need to accept. Alcohol does not make you smarter, funnier, more athletic, better looking, stronger or taller.

Sometimes people drink to give themselves the nerve to say something they want to get off their chest. Too late, they realize silence is better than incoherence. Some people drink to forget, and then find themselves doing even more things they need to forget.

36

· In moderation, alcohol can enhance a friendship, a romance or an event. In excess, somebody ends up running down the street with no shirt on while their home burns in the background.

But alcohol is particularly dangerous during courtship as it can throw off the way signals are sent and received and skew the results (*skew* is not a typo). Here are a few guidelines to prevent alcohol from ruining your relationship:

- Your alcohol consumption makes her prettier and you uglier.
- Know your limit. If you can't say the word <u>chrysanthemum</u>, stop drinking. If you <u>can</u> say it but do so for no reason, that's no better.
- Never be more than one drink ahead of your date. If she's had two, stop at three. If she's had one, stop at two. If she doesn't drink, ask to meet her friends.
- Use alcohol to help celebrate a decision, not to help <u>make</u> one.
- It's a bad plan to try to get her drunk so she'll sleep with you. It's an even worse plan to get yourself drunk so <u>you'll</u> sleep with <u>her</u>.
- Make sure this is the girl for you before you start drinking. People who don't like each other sober don't usually change their minds after a six-pack.
- If you need alcohol to make her attractive the night before, how's she going to look in the morning when you're hungover?
- Alcohol kills brain cells. You have none to spare.
- Don't abuse alcohol now, while you're young and full of life. Save it until you've been married thirty years and could really use it.
- The big risk of drinking is that you will say something intelligent but nobody will take you seriously. Whereas saying dumb things while you're sober is better for everybody.

- Love is like a car. You can get it started with alcohol, but it won't run for long.

GOOD CRAZY, BAD CRAZY, CRAZY CRAZY

I think most people accept that being crazy is often a good thing. It can have a romantic meaning, like "That guy is crazy about you," or it can describe somebody who's fun to be with, like "I had a crazy time with that guy," or it can mean something a little darker, like "That guy is psychotic and should be locked up." So what we have are three different kinds of crazy: good crazy, bad crazy and crazy crazy. If you're trying to get a girl to like you, you want to make sure you stay within the parameters of good crazy. This is the crazy that makes women fall in love. It's the one they write country songs about. Bad crazy is the kind your buddies might get a kick out of on the way home from the football game, but it rarely works with women. Crazy crazy is the kind that scares people and requires professional help to correct. It's important that you be able to categorize your crazy notions while they're still in the planning stages, rather than waiting until the deed is done and the cops are pulling into the driveway. You don't want to be boring, but you need to be the right kind of crazy. Here are some examples:

Good Crazy: You put a full, steaming hot tub in the back of your pickup truck and drive over to your girlfriend's house.

Bad Crazy: You put a full, steaming hot tub in the back of your pickup truck and drive over to your girlfriend's house naked.

Crazy Crazy: You put a full, steaming hot tub in the back of your pickup truck and drive over to your girlfriend's house naked—*and* the hot tub is chock full of sliced vegetables and chunks of beef and one giant crouton in the shape of an armadillo.

Good Crazy: You pick her up for a date but instead whisk her off to Vegas for the weekend.

Bad Crazy: You pick her up for a date but instead whisk her off to Schenectady for two weeks.

Crazy Crazy: You pick her up for a date but instead whisk her off to a minimum-security prison for six months less a day.

Good Crazy: You take your fiancée to a seafood restaurant and get an unemployed captain to marry the two of you in the parking lot.

Bad Crazy: You take your fiancée to a machine shop and have your rings welded together while you're wearing them.

Crazy Crazy: You take your fiancée to an abattoir, where the minister butchers the ceremony, the candles are kielbasa, the organ is a kidney and the pew is unbearable.

HER FACE COMES TO YOUR PLACE

After you've been dating for a while and you've seen all the current movies and have gone out for dinner with her so many times you've met every cashier at the drive-thru, it will be time to invite her over to your apartment for a stay-at-home date.

This is a pivotal evening for the relationship. It may be hard to believe, but when a single girl visits a guy in his pad, he's a lot more vulnerable than she is. That's because she's going to learn a whole lot about him. Way more than he realizes, and way, *way* more than he'd like her to. So you've got to prepare for that by taking some extra steps to make sure she doesn't learn too much about you too soon.

The visit starts when she arrives and parks her car. Meet her in the parking lot so you can walk her into the building. If there's an old smelly guy who sleeps in the foyer, come in through the back door. And you accompanying her saves that awkward moment when she buzzes up to be let in and you can't understand each other because of that time you spilled a rye and ginger into the intercom and now everyone's voice sounds like somebody speaking Chinese through a box of tinfoil.

If the elevator is shaky, take the stairs and save it for when she's leaving. Even bad elevators can usually go down okay. If necessary, dress up the outside of your apartment door a little. Maybe a welcome sign or some seasonal message that you can use to hide the holes from the fire axe. Or just leave the door open—a subtle way of saying you trust your neighbours, even if the truth is they would never steal from you because their stuff is way nicer than yours.

Her first step into your apartment is crucial. She needs to be stepping on the floor—not a sock or newspaper or a laundry bag or a hamster. The place needs to look clean and tidy. And it needs to have either no smell or a good smell. There's a way of wedging an aerosol air freshener into the workings of a clock so that it sprays a blast of lotus blossom delight every hour on the hour.

Put some thought into what you have sitting on the tables and hanging on the walls. No weapons. Especially no guns. Especially no smoking guns. If you have awards, frame them and hang them prominently. Even if they're just for attendance, they show you've been places. Have family pictures on display. It doesn't have to be *your* family, just *some* family. She won't care at this point. If you have a picture of her, display it prominently—and nowhere near the dartboard.

If your couch is a sofa bed, make sure it's in the sofa configuration. Have the dinner already made and keeping warm in the oven. Just buy it all to go from a local restaurant and then ask your neighbour how to turn the oven on. Do not under any circumstances attempt to clean the bathroom yourself. It's too big a job and you obviously have no experience at it. You need to hire a professional heavy-industrial cleaning company that has a detox specialist. You should really have them clean the entire apartment, but you can't afford that, so just have them do the bathroom and with the money you save, you can buy dimmers.

The main thing is to just be yourself. Or not. It might actually be better for you to be somebody else. Somebody calmer. Someone with no expectations. You've gotta just appreciate her being there and let her take the lead. Don't slip away for a moment and come back wearing pyjamas. Or even worse, not wearing pyjamas. And don't try to get her all liquored up. Assume she'll be driving home in a few hours and you need her to be able to do that safely. You, however, aren't going anywhere, so you can pound it back like Blackbeard on shore leave.

The key to your future is showing your appreciation for her being there. Or for just being. Or for nothing. Even undeserved appreciation makes most men irresistible.

LIKE FATHER, LIKE HELL

You'll probably find that your new girlfriend is adjusting smoothly to your world, in terms of activities you like to do and the friends and family you like to do them with. But remember, the seriousness of your relationship with this girl is directly proportional to the scrutiny you are under.

The more you like her and want to be with her, the more she's going to expect you to change. And the most pivotal moment of that evolution occurs when she has just accepted your marriage proposal and then meets your father for the first time. Chances are she will be mortified. She'll meet this fat, old, snarly guy who has no social graces and considers himself the centre of the universe.

On the surface, she'll be challenged by the thought of having to deal with this regularly now that she's joining the family. But her biggest concern is that you will one day turn into this guy. Unzipping your pants after a big meal, sleeping on the recliner, crabbing about everything from the price of hammers to the way the neighbour walks, and emanating more bizarre body noises than C3PO.

If you're not adopted, then you are genetically programmed to be just like him. Plus you have been raised in his environment and have come to accept his behaviour as normal.

You're going to have to abandon all of that. There is no way on earth she is going to allow you to become your father. She may even write it into the marriage vows. She'll get you to stop smoking cigars and then stop smoking cigarettes and then stop smoking altogether. She will change your diet to prevent you from doubling your body weight every ten years. She'll put you on a tough-love program that directly connects your behaviour to her rewards. She'll become an expert on what you like and then withhold that to motivate you to become the best you can be. Or at least, better than your dad.

And friends and family who know your dad will be on her side. So just do what you gotta do and stop your whining.

Don't get me wrong, it doesn't mean that this is a completely one-sided process. Because chances are you're going to face the same problem with her that she's facing with you. And you'll be aware of that similarity the moment you meet her mother. And the moment you become aware of how her mother treats her father. This is not a future you will find appealing. But it does level the playing field and give you a bargaining position. You can sit your fiancée down and admit that it would be better for everyone if you don't turn into your father, but that it would also give your marriage the best chance for success if she doesn't turn into her mother. That may be a tough one, but it needs to be said.

I know we should all show gratitude to our parents, but that doesn't mean we need to duplicate them. Mother Nature is like

Bill Gates. The next generation always needs to be The Parents Version 2.0.

MEETING HER FATHER

There is no more crucial step in the development of this relationship than the first time you meet her father. This guy is your school principal, judge, jury and parole officer, all in one. With one difference: those people are all impartial; this guy is not. He's assuming you're a loser, and it'll be hard to get him to change his mind. Especially if you *are* a loser.

This man sees every suitor as his daughter's highway to a good life, and right now he's looking at you like you're a cul-de-sac. The first step in overcoming that perception is for you to treat him with great respect, even if nobody else in the world, even his own family, does. Call him sir, but don't overdo it. Adding the name "Lancelot" removes all the sincerity.

If every one of this guy's friends are smart asses, that doesn't allow you to be one. He's not looking to be your friend. In his mind, you're trying to take away the only woman in the world he has truly gotten along with.

In golf they have a shot called the "son-in-law"—the translation is "not quite what I had in mind." You're fighting an uphill battle, so I suggest a quiet war. Don't talk much. Don't introduce controversial subjects. Let him do that and then wait until he clearly defines his position.

But don't be quick to agree with him, or you'll alienate your girlfriend's mother. Just do a few *I sees* and *interestings*. You may not like to be a fence-sitter but 99 per cent of the time, wishy-washy wins. I would say you should forget about getting her father to like you and instead concentrate on getting him to feel comfortable around you. To do that, you need to avoid dead air.

There's nothing worse than an uncomfortable silence. It implies that you have nothing in common or will only start an argument by speaking or that maybe each of you is thinking the other person doesn't have enough intelligence to comprehend or respond—and, sadly, you both may be right.

You need to find a way to fill the dead air. It's one of the reasons professional sport was created. Turn on the NFL and crank up the volume. Watch to see which team he's cheering for and join him. If there's no game on or the cable's been cut off because of a misunderstanding over what happens when you don't pay your bill, you may have to rely on conversation. That's a minefield. Especially if it's just the two of you trying to talk. You both hate making small talk. And big talk always leads to a fistfight. You might think bringing your girlfriend and her mother into the conversation would help, but that only gives you a glimpse into how this guy treats his wife, and you may not be able to hold your tongue.

The best solution to all of these problems is for you to only spend time with her father when you're on your way to do something else. Something with a deadline—like a flight you have to catch or a doctor's appointment or a court appearance. Never drop in on your way home because you won't be able to leave without being rude and, although you enjoy being rude, it doesn't lead to him giving you his daughter anytime soon.

So be respectful, keep the visits short, and if you can't think of anything, don't say it.

BATTING ORDER FOR RELATIVES

In the challenge to land the woman of your dreams, your relatives can be very helpful in persuading her she could do a lot worse. But it doesn't just happen; you have to orchestrate it. For example, the order in which she meets your relatives needs to be geared to the development of your relationship. You need to manage that sequence, like the manager of a baseball team. And also like a manager, you need to draw up your most effective batting order.

Leadoff hitter: Mom. Your mother is the perfect person to convince your girlfriend that you are lovable and that you enjoy being mothered. This initial message can set you up for a lifetime of nurturing. Mothers never strike out, and *you'll* get to first base.

Batting second: Sis. Even if your sister doesn't like you, her mere presence implies that you are capable of cohabitating with a woman who shares your status in the family. She will probably go down swinging, but be kind to her and you'll look like a champ.

Batting third: Grandma. Your grandmother is a great opportunity to show what a nice guy you are. Any man who is nice to his grandmother gets a lot of points. But don't expect too much from the at-bat. Your grandmother stopped swinging years ago.

(You'll notice the first three batters are women. That's not a fluke. Your girlfriend will be impressed if you have even a half-decent relationship with these three diverse women in your life. It will make her optimistic about your long-term potential and so increase her commitment to the relationship and allow you to bring in your next three batters.)

Batting fourth: your best friend. I don't mean the guy who is your best friend. I mean a friend of yours who is the best person you know. A kind, sensitive person, good-looking, smart, successful and fit. She will subliminally assign those characteristics to you, simply because you associate with this guy. She may also regret having hooked up with you before she met him, but chances are he's gay.

Batting fifth: your boss. Here again, it's a subtle message. Your girlfriend is meeting a successful businessman who sifted through a number of job applicants and ultimately chose you. It's exactly what you're asking her to do, and for once she'll appreciate not being the first.

Batting sixth: your finance company rep. This is the person who lent you the money to buy that used Hummer. He obviously saw something in you that was honest and responsible. It will make your girlfriend feel better about you to know that this person trusts you. And it will make this person feel better to know that your girlfriend might help pay back the loan.

(By this point, you've covered the bases. You've shown your ability to build personal and business relationships. Your girlfriend is now as committed to you as she's ever going to be. It's time to show her the dark side of the batting order.)

Batting seventh: your best friend. This time I mean it. Your *actual* best friend. The guy you drink beer with and go to monster truck rallies with. He may be a little rough around the edges. He may be missing a few teeth—and several brains. His language may be salty and his stories about you may be as inappropriate as they are true. Your girlfriend won't like him. She'll think he's not good enough for you. You'll defend him and say you would never turn your back on your best friend. But you will if you have to.

Batting eighth: your brother. This is the guy who knows absolutely every embarrassing moment of your life and can't wait to share each and every one of them with your sweetheart. Let him. While she's there, just let him say whatever he wants and hang your head in embarrassment. It'll make you pathetic and lovable. After she goes, you can give your brother a wedgie that borders on gender-reassignment surgery.

Batting ninth, the cleanup hitter: Dad. For your girlfriend, this is potentially the Ghost of Christmas Future. She'll see him sitting at the head of the table in his underwear, blaming the immigration policies for his inability to secure a senior management position or get his Grade 10.

While his very existence will scare your girlfriend, for you it will create an absolute worst-case scenario. She will be so thankful that you are so much better than your dad, she will be hesitant to criticize any of your imperfections.

(There is nothing better than family to recalibrate the instruments of any couple. And it works for both sides. Whenever you lose the love or even attraction for each other, make an effort to spend more time with each other's families and you'll see how lucky you both are.)

THE CARE PACKAGE

The average man and the average woman care about entirely different things. It's very difficult to find common ground when your priorities are that far out of sync. But it all starts with learning what those differences are. See the following graph:

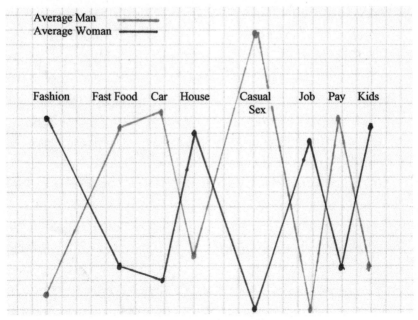

MARRYING A MODEL

It's probably every man's dream to marry a model—or maybe even a supermodel, but then you'd have to be Super*man*. So I thought it might be important to help you look at the big picture in language you can understand.

First of all, let's look at the word *model*. It sometimes means "miniature version of the real thing," but I'm sure that's not what you're looking for. You want the full-sized real thing, and you may even want some areas as large as possible. The other and more applicable meaning of *model* is "ideal." This is the ultimate physical version of a human being. Perfect face, perfect hair, perfect body, perfect everything.

Yes, you'd like to have a woman like that hanging on your arm, but that's only natural. Your instincts are all telling you this is a good thing—a very, very good thing. And maybe it is, but you need to think about it.

Let's start with how you look. Are you a male model? Are you even an "artist's rendering" of a male? You're attracted to this model because she's flawless, but how flawless are you? In contrast, are you actually flaw-full? Try to imagine how the two of you are going to look together. Her beauty will not enhance your ugliness. Quite the opposite: she'll look like an exquisite statue and you'll look like the packing crate. Strangers who see you together will assume it's an arranged marriage. Or they may think you must be incredibly wealthy, which is fine for about a minute and then they'll start asking you for money.

And think about what your wife's life will be like. If enough people tell her how ridiculous it is for her to be married to you, she may eventually agree with them. That makes you vulnerable. You already have enough of that in your life.

Let me give you another perspective. When you go to buy a car, they have the ones for sale out in the lot, but they have the "model" in the showroom. That's because the model is not only the best-looking and most fully loaded, it also gets the best treatment. It's not out in the elements. It gets groomed and buffed every day. Nobody takes the model off-road or uses it to pick up a yard of manure. If they do, it doesn't stay a model for long.

It's the same thing with your model wife. Yes, she may have beauty, but beauty is a commitment. It requires constant vigilance and maintenance. Those hands can't be washing dishes or carrying lumber or torquing a head bolt. That hair can't be full of plaster dust. Those legs are too great to be lifting furniture. When you marry a model, you become the custodian of a rare collectible and it's your duty to men everywhere to do everything you can to keep that specimen in showroom condition.

And don't assume that once you get to the bedroom it'll all be worth it. Models need their sleep. Don't get me wrong: I'm not saying don't marry a model. I'm just saying you need to think about all of the things you have to sacrifice to sustain her in the lifestyle to which she has become accustomed. I'd hate to see you marry somebody just for their looks and then your eyes go.

FREE LOVE?

Every person has a computer inside their brain. Some have the NASA genius model, some have a Commodore 64. But even the most basic of these computers is preloaded with software that programs you to walk upright, communicate, eat over the sink, and reproduce. And as annoying as eating over the sink can be to everyone else at the restaurant, the drive to reproduce is the one that causes the problems.

Generally, girls, as potential mothers, are very aware of these natural urges but are equally aware of the consequences. Whereas boys, as potential fathers, are focused on the urges alone, and dismiss the consequences as something that won't happen for at least nine months—and even then, it will be to somebody else.

Boys find out at an early age that when you consider the consequences of your actions before doing them, it takes all the fun out of life. They would never have slalomed on a skateboard being towed by a pickup truck. They would never have dived off a neighbour's roof into what, up until the moment of impact, was an above-ground pool. They would never have eaten forty-three pickled eggs on the first night of a camping trip.

Many of the great discoveries and scientific breakthroughs in history have come from somebody, usually a man, not considering the consequences. So it's usually up to the girl to keep everything in perspective. It's a pattern you see throughout life—the women do the thinking for both of them. The men *can* think—they just prefer not to.

Now, I know they have modern preventative medicine and accessories that make children inconceivable, but even if you take the risk of pregnancy out of the equation, getting intimate changes everything. Whether you call it "lovemaking" or "shagging" or "doin' the humpty-hump" or "taking one for the team," it moves the relationship to a different level.

When you start going steady, it's like you join a very selective club that has the two of you as its only members. At first you're a silver member, which gives you exclusive dating privileges, as well as kissing, hugging and hand holding. As long as you live up to your responsibilities as a silver cardholder over a period of time determined by your girlfriend, you will be upgraded to a gold membership, which allows all the privileges of silver but adds bonus features like extended wet kisses, show and tell, and the popular touchy-feely. A gold-level member gets to participate in every aspect of the baseball game with the exception of the home run.

To clear the bases, you need to be a platinum member, which can take months of fidelity and service and just the correct amount of begging. But if and when you ever do get that home run, your life changes at that moment—or, more accurately, at that second. Your girlfriend would only be that intimate with someone she was planning to spend the rest of her life with and you, as a platinum member, are saying you feel the same way. Right? Right??

It can be a problem pretending to feel things you don't. Most guys think that if they get enough sex it might lead to love, but the girl is thinking the exact opposite. So whether or not you feel she is the long-term one for you, once you empty the bases, you have to at least pretend you feel that way, in the hope that one day you will.

So there are a lot of responsibilities and expectations that come with a platinum card, but getting it on with the girl of your dreams proves once and for all that membership has its privileges.

OPPOSITES SUBTRACT

There's an old wives' tale that people who have opposite personalities and characteristics are often attracted to each other, and while it may work for old wives, I think in general that's a lot of baloney.

A woman is not "attracted to" her opposite. She may be "intrigued by" or "curious about" or "too horrified to look away," but equating that to attraction is a big mistake. It seems unlikely to me that a soft-spoken career librarian would be attracted to an overbearing loud carny who spends his weekends being shot out of a cannon into a vat of yogurt.

Sure, you may take special notice of a person who is unlike anything you've ever experienced, but that has more to do with the instinct for self-preservation than it does with your innate need for adventure. In the short term, a couple who are radically different from each other will have some interesting experiences together that they may even regard as fun, like the way you remember the first time you rode a mechanical bull or ate haggis, but over the long haul their chances of compatibility are incredibly slim.

That's because the differences are not superficial, they're deep. It's not that one person went out and discovered helicopter bungee jumping and the other person didn't. They were both aware of the same activities. One said no. The other said yes. This is not a trivial difference. This is about fundamental life choices. Or death choices. While it may be kind of sexy to be married to a guy who jumps out of airplanes with nothing but a cape and an air mattress, this is probably not the person you want making key family decisions. That's what ruins it.

The kind of person you are determines the kinds of decisions you make. Most people are happy with their decisions. If they're not, they change them. So when you meet someone who makes totally different decisions than you do, it's pretty much impossible that you agree with those decisions. Sometimes these adventurers don't even make decisions, they just never say no. To anything. In my experience, sooner or later people who never say no end up saying goodbye. Sometimes to everybody.

So if you think you're attracted to somebody who's the opposite of you, stop and think for a minute. Is it actually envy? Jealous of a person who makes much braver choices than you do? Don't be fooled; these may not be brave choices for them. Maybe they don't even think about that. Or about anything. Maybe you're angry that stupid people seem to have more fun. Whatever it is, it probably isn't love.

You're way better off to find someone who makes the same kinds of decisions you do. Go back to the library, where you'll be able to find a soulmate. The adventurer will find *his* in the emergency room.

BREAKING UP WITHOUT BREAKING DOWN

It's very unlikely that the first girl you date is going to end up as a lifelong love connection. Compatibility is not that easy. She's going to have things about her that you don't like, and we all know you have things about you that *nobody* likes. At first, the things you like about each other dominate the other stuff. But over time, you take the good things for granted, which makes the bad things really bug you.

So eventually the time comes when you need to break up. It's tricky. It has to end, but the goal is for it to end in a way that allows each person to get on with their lives. That requires a little extra care in the way the breakup is handled. You also need to consider what level of breakup this is, because the depth and duration of the relationship very much affects the game plan for blowing it out of the water.

Let's start with the easiest breakup of all. This is the one where you've had one or two lacklustre dates and you've got the feeling that this girl never wants to go out with you again because after the last date, she said, "I never want to go out with you again." So there's no point in trying to save this relationship. However, you need to save face. You don't want your friends to think you're a pathetic loser. Hopefully, it's not too late. You need to wait until the girl is standing with a bunch of her friends, and then walk over with a bunch of your friends and casually break up with her. Say something like "I can't do this anymore, Samantha. I need to be with somebody who cares about me. And it's clearly not you. So get stuffed."

Don't say it exactly that way, especially if her name isn't Samantha. But the idea is you're pre-empting her. She may have been polite by breaking up with you privately, but now you get the last laugh by breaking up with her publicly. Both your friends and her friends will think you're something. Maybe even something good.

The next level of breaking up is when you've been dating for a while and it's been getting more serious and to the untrained eye, like hers, it might even have looked as though you were on the path to marriage. This one is a little trickier. It's going to be hard for you to come off well. She thought she was the one. Now she's not even one of the ones. You've got to break up with her in such a way that she ends up feeling good about it. You don't want her to hurt herself, and you sure don't want her to hurt you.

Some people will advise you to tell the truth. I'm not one of them. However, I would say you should avoid a really bad lie. Avoid clichés of any kind. Don't ever say, "It's not you, it's me." That's not true. It's not you, it's *her*. If she were somebody else, somebody nicer and better-looking, you wouldn't be breaking up. And don't say, "You're just not ready." Okay, maybe it's not a lie, but it's not the whole truth, either. You'll never be ready. Not for her.

I should mention that if you're moving to another country and never coming back, you could tell her you're gay. Just don't expect her to be surprised.

But if you're planning on staying in town and seeing other people, you need a clean break with no carry-over. My advice is for you to tell her that you have always dreamed of meeting a girl who means everything to you, that you would do anything for, that you would die for, and that you know there's somebody out there who will feel that way about her, but it's not you. Bummer. Then hang up.

If you're at the third level of ending a relationship, you have to take your game up a notch or two. At this point, you're engaged. That means you've made a commitment and plans have been made based on that commitment. Wedding plans. Housing plans. Parenting plans. And the person who's made those plans is going to want to kill you. That person is your fiancée's mother. Your fiancée's father won't give you any problems at all. He can under- stand why a man would change his mind about getting married, and your breakup is going to save him 50 Gs in wedding costs. However, his support will only hurt him and not help you.

You've really complicated the issue because you've let this go way too long. You are now trying to return after crossing the point of no return. No one does that. That's why they call it the point of no return. Your only realistic explanation of your change in heart is the "pursuit of happiness." At this moment, nobody gives a rat's butt about your happiness. However there will be pursuit if you try to weasel out of the wedding. The bride is so committed to this thing, she'd rather marry somebody who didn't love her than call off the wedding or return the shower gifts.

This is not a time for rational explanation. This is a time for radical action. You put a lot of effort into proving to this girl and her family that you were worthy to ask for her hand. Now you have to put at least that much effort into convincing them of the complete opposite. This is a time to be irrational and unreliable. Quit your job. Max out your credit cards and go to Sandals by yourself. Stop returning phone calls and emails from your girl-friend. Find pictures of men in compromising situations, then Photoshop your head on their bodies and post the photos on the Internet. Ask the girl's father to lend you $500,000 to start a singles' club and then send him a strip-o-gram to sweeten the deal. Recommend him and his wife as potential Amway dealers. You need to focus on making their family life a living hell so that they will force their daughter to call off the wedding and all of them will feel like they dodged a bullet. You.

THE 18,000-NIGHT STAND

Men like to brag to each other about their success with the ladies. They like to describe every detail of their latest con-quest, even if it's imaginary. That's because men equate their manliness to their sexual proclivity. And they don't mind implying that a woman found them attractive enough to qualify and yet was still sober enough to be aware of what she was doing.

We've all heard of the track records of big movie stars—and of professional athletes, with their ability to do most of their scoring long after the game is over. It seems the more one-night stands you've had, the more of a man you are. It doesn't carry the same badge of honour for a woman. That's probably a sign of inequality, but I don't think it's fair for women to change now that I'm long past my Don Juan phase.

In any case, I have a whole different perspective. You might think it's impressive for a guy to have had 18,000 one-night stands in his life, but I think it's a lot more significant to have one 18,000-night stand. That's a fifty-year marriage. To the same woman.

Spending 18,000 nights with the same woman has got to be a lot harder than spending one night with 18,000 different women. They never find you boring or repetitive. You can surprise anybody one night at a time. I've even heard guys say that after a one-night stand they're anxious for her to grab a cab and get outta there. If she stays for the weekend, that really puts a strain on things, and if they go away for a week together, they run out of things to do and say. They'd never be able to tough it out for fifty years.

It's hard not to run out of new things to do and say. In fact, it's impossible. My wife and I ran out about twenty years ago. Thank God for news, sports and weather or we'd be sitting in a rubber room talking along with each other by now.

At this point we've said it all and done it all. Is that boring? Yes. But boring is not necessarily a bad thing. Nobody ever stubbed a toe or broke an arm or threw out a back from boredom. Sure, they might have done those things from their reaction to boredom, but it wasn't the boredom itself. As you get older, you will begin to embrace boredom. It's quiet and peaceful and it doesn't expect you to do anything.

What I'm getting at here is your ability to discover, and subsequently enjoy, a comfort level with that special person in your life. You don't get that from a one-night stand. A one-night stand may give you excitement, maybe pleasure, maybe even pride, but not comfort. There's no comfort in a one-night stand, especially if she stays for breakfast.

Comfort is the long-term prize, and to get it you've got to go way past a one-night stand.

There are a lot of women in this world who will excite you, but there are probably only a couple that will make you feel comfortable. Grab one of them and string as many one-night stands together as both of you can stand together.

COUPLING

If you look at the human body, you'll notice that everything is supposed to be symmetrical. You have two of almost everything— eyes, ears, arms, legs, etc.—and there's one on each side. If you only have one of something—nose, mouth, belly button, etc.—it's in the middle, unless you've been in an unfortunate accident or have very bad posture. So it's natural for each of us to try to find symmetry in other parts of our lives.

That's why, when you go from being a single person to becoming a couple, it is no longer okay for you as a couple to hang out with a single person, no matter how much you like them. Because it's awkward. The math doesn't work. Somebody's outnumbered. The balance is gone. When you and your wife go out for lunch with one of her girlfriends, do you let them just talk about girly stuff while you sit there making up cartoons in your head? Are you allowed to talk at all? Can you make jokes? What kind of jokes? Surely not those double-entendre sexual references, like saying "under the covers" after every item on the menu, that you and the guys find hilarious. No. No way. Because you have no backup. No other guy there to laugh and get you off the hook, or at least share the disgust.

And can you just lean over and kiss your wife if you feel like it? No chance. Not with her girlfriend there. What's she supposed to do? Look away like it didn't happen? And if there's a band playing, can you get up and dance with your wife? She's not going to go for that. That's being rude to her girlfriend. So are you supposed to dance with the girlfriend? No, you're not, and I can vouch for that. I guess if it's a Greek restaurant you can dance with both of them at once, but that will be more attention than you want.

And what about when the bill comes? Do you split it with the girlfriend? Do you each pay for your own? Or do you just pick up the tab for everyone? Of course you do and you're gracious about it, but you sure don't *feel* gracious about it. That's because couples and singles are like oil and water. They don't mix—one kind of floats on top of the other and nobody feels like going swimming.

And it's not any better when you, your wife and your buddy go to a ball game. Your wife is uncomfortable. She feels like an outsider. Sure, you can have her go to the snack bar to get you and Bob a beer, but that gets old after the sixth or seventh trip. After a while she will stop even trying to be part of the conversation and will refuse to do the wave.

And it's not the event. A couple and a single socializing together just plain does not work. Singles need to be with singles. Couples need to be with couples. It's nature's way. It doesn't mean that once you're a couple, you can't see your buddies and she can't see her girlfriends. You just have to isolate the activities. The two of you need to realize this.

Once in a while she needs to just be with her girlfriends and you need to just be with your buddies. And those things need to happen simultaneously. That way you turn a potential negative into a welcome break from each other that allows you to renew your relationship. Just make sure the one who needs the break the least gets to decide on the frequency of these timeouts. If your wife is happy to see her girlfriends three or four times a year but you want to spend every Sunday with your buddies, that will be a problem. Initially it will be *her* problem, but eventually, as it grows in size and intensity, it will be *your* problem.

Just accept it. You're a couple now. Look up *couple* in the dictionary and you won't see you and your buddy at the Super Bowl. You'll need a thesaurus for that.

I know this is tough for you to hear, but there is a silver lining in this for both of you. If you can't find a couple that you want to spend time with, maybe you can build one. Just imagine if you could hook up your favourite single buddy with your wife's favourite single girlfriend. Would that not be the greatest solution ever? You'd have the best of all possible worlds. You'd be seeing each other as couples and as single friends, all at the same time. Okay, maybe it's a long shot that they'd find a love connection, but so what? Even if they're barely compatible, you've got to convince them to get married. That's what friends are for.

TRYING TO MAKE WORK RELATIONSHIPS WORK

In the old days, most men would meet their life partners at high school. There are plenty of reasons for this: there were lots of girls there, and most of them weren't married; it was easy and convenient (and so were some of the girls); and the guys who spent seven years or more in high school had that much more time to meet a bride.

But times have changed. People don't get married young anymore, largely due to a general rejection of shotgun weddings. So now men have to look elsewhere to find that special woman. Yes, you could meet a woman at your favourite bar, but then you'd be marrying someone who has the same character flaws as you, and that's not how a species evolves. The other tempting location to find a life partner is at your place of work. You see the person every day. You can start with short conversations, maybe bring them a coffee at break time, eventually have your lunches together and then let it escalate from there.

Let me just say from the outset that this is a huge mistake. When you date someone from work, one of you will eventually have to find another job. There are just too many obstacles and too much togetherness. For most marriages, the only way to keep people together is to keep them apart. But even putting the too-much-togetherness issue aside, there are so many other things that can happen at work that will put the relationship at risk. Let's say, for example, that both you and your girlfriend have similar jobs at the company. What if you get a promotion and she doesn't? Or more likely, what if she gets a promotion and you don't? What if she becomes your boss? How would you feel about sleeping with your boss? Okay, maybe that's a bad example, but you get the idea. And how would the other workers feel about your wife being the boss? She wouldn't ever be able to give you a raise or a commendation. She'd have to just reward you at home. Okay, maybe that's another bad example, but you know what I mean. It's just way too complicated when the two of you work at the same place. Even if you're in completely separate depart-ments. Every company has a grapevine, and your wife would find out right away that you were caught sleeping in the back of the warehouse. But sometimes I know it just happens where you meet the person at work and it's magic and you both fall in love and want to be together forever.

As the man, you're the one who's going to have to step up. Explain to your fiancée that working together will put the mar-riage in jeopardy and hurt both of your careers and you just couldn't live with yourself if you did that. So instead, you will quit your job and stay home to look after the kids who may or may not come along one day. It's a big sacrifice, but you might just be man enough to do it.

WIFE WANTED

If you're having trouble finding a wife and you're getting frustrated because you think it should be easy, it might help you to step back and take a look at what you're asking for and what you're offering in return. To help explain what I mean, I've prepared the following job description. Take a look at it and imagine it as a job posting at your local employment agency. If you were a prospective bride, would you be interested?

POSITION AVAILABLE
- Eligible bachelor looking for wife.
- Applicant must be young, attractive and personable.
- Full time position—24/7. For life.
- Duties include cooking, cleaning, laundry, intimacy, birthing, breastfeeding, nursing, parenting and assorted household chores.
- Successful applicant will be expected to also have a well-paying job outside the home.
- Remuneration will be on a profit-sharing basis. Wife will contribute her entire income to the central fund and will then share in any profits once all household bills have been paid.
- Engager is offering 50 per cent partnership position, redeemable through divorce or death.
- Retirement is not an option.
- Days off will be determined through mutual agreement or marital argument.

- Employment will commence with official ceremony (wedding) followed by celebratory welcome-aboard party (reception). Size and duration of party to be based on what the applicant's father can afford.
- Equal-opportunity employer.
- Female lawyers need not apply.

You'll never have to worry if your bride loves you. She must if she's taking *that* job.

ANOTHER WORLD

Before you get too far along towards your goal of closing the deal on a life partner, you have to realize that you're not just adding a person to your life, you're adding a world. The fully realized adult human being ends up living in five different worlds and, although you live in them simultaneously, it is very dangerous to have any two of them collide.

The first world is yourself. This is the person you know the best and have spent the most time with. There are things you say and do, to and for this person, that you would never say or do to or for any other human being. You have many thoughts that you never share, which is good because it allows you to keep friends and stay out of prison. Your own self is the first world you arrive in and the last one you leave. It is the world of your ego and, although very important, it needs to be a home base from which to explore other worlds. Historically, men who remain in this first world have bizarre lives—Robinson Crusoe, Tarzan, Donald Trump.

The second world is your family. You treat your family differently than anyone else in the world. They created you, fed you, clothed you, educated you, disciplined you and empowered you. They are your investors. When you're talking to your family, you're talking to your shareholders. They don't think it's funny that you never pay your parking tickets and have a beer keg in your bedroom. You have to keep reassuring your family that everything's fine. Keep reminding them of other great people who struggled early and then finally made it. Make Colonel Sanders your role model. That will buy you time and keep the investors investing. If you stop here at the two-world mark, you'll be a lifetime victim of arrested development and never reach your true potential. Remember the Cartwrights from *Bonanza*? If you're too young, just think of the Kardashians but without the dress code and fake weddings.

The third world is your friends. Actions and opinions that your family finds disgusting, your friends find entertaining. As the ultimate compliment, when you do something incredibly stupid, instead of criticizing, your friends will attempt to top it. And sadly, you encourage each other. Whenever you hear about some prank that involves alcohol, nudity and the principal's car being found on the roof of the gymnasium, it's rarely the product of one kid working alone. This third world is the most dangerous because there's no "voice of reason." That's why, when the cops ask the bunch of you why you packed the school bus heater with pig manure, there's no voice of reason. Heck, after ten minutes on the bus, there's barely a voice.

The fourth world is optional. It's made up of your business associates. It's optional because to live in that world you have to have a job where you work with other people. Ranger Gord does not live in that world. Or, in fact, in any of these worlds. But if you're lucky enough to have that kind of job, you know that you have to watch yourself to keep it. You don't want your boss to see you at Hooters. Especially if his daughter works there. You have to put on airs with these people. These are not the same as your friends. You can't tell these people the funny jokes. Just the clean ones.

And now you're contemplating adding a fifth world to this menagerie. Because once you find this girl and start courting her, you will say and do things that you've never said or done in any of the other worlds. If all goes well, it will be the best world yet and there will be a temptation to abandon the other worlds and just live in this one. Don't do it. She may want to be the most important thing in your world, but she doesn't want to get there by being the *only* thing in your world. She wants you to have plenty of choices and to pick her, rather than just set her as your default. And it doesn't make you a better person by excluding yourself, your family, your friends and your workmates. Instead, it makes you a weasly little pathetic, spineless love slave, working 24/7 and being paid with sex. And when you get older you won't even be able to cash the cheques.

But it's not enough to keep all the worlds—you have to keep all the worlds *apart*. You can't go out with your buddies and bring your girlfriend along. You can't have your workmates go bowling with your family. Even mixing your girlfriend in with your family is dangerous and something that should only be done on special occasions like Christmas or whenever your family is mad at you. To me, the perfect day is when you go to work and have a few laughs with the crew, take your mom out for lunch, have a beer with your buddies after work, be home for dinner and the evening with your sweetheart, then set your internal alarm for 2 a.m. so you can wake up and think about things. Just make sure you don't wake her up. Unless you want to.

BUYER'S REMORSE

You've been going steady for a while. You have shared a lot of your secrets and have made a bunch of good and bad discoveries about each other. You are no longer seen as two individuals. You are what they call an "item." But just like in a department store, there are lots of different kinds of items. There are good-quality items, there are poor-quality items, there are damaged items, there are even discontinued items. What you won't find are items sitting on the display rack for years on end.

Being an item means you're farther along than just dating, but you're still in a transitional phase. And someday soon you will be faced with the question of how much longer this relationship will go on. You'd like that day to be about ten years away. Your girlfriend was thinking this Friday. Her father was thinking *last* Friday.

You might think it's a lot easier to make a commitment now than it was when you barely knew each other. It's not. You can't imagine how something looks once you've seen it. Reality is the hardest thing in the world to base a decision on. That's the whole appeal of blind dates. Everything's great up until you open that front door.

The best option, of course, is to not make a decision at all. That's the manly way. But you've been doing that for a year and you've just been notified that not everyone in the relationship is really pleased with the status quo. So with Plan A being a non-starter, you have three options left:

Plan B: Get more intertwined. Move in together. Propose marriage. Propose something somewhat resembling marriage. Whatever happens, it will be an indication to her, her friends, her family—her father—that this thing continues to move forward towards the inevitable goal of the two of you living together as man and wife, or at least as man and woman.

Plan C: Take a break. A defined period during which each of you can step back for a few months and not see each other. You can date other people and have total freedom and then, when the three months is done, you will know if this is the perfect partner for you. When this idea is presented, it has to be done in a carefully worded, clear, impersonal voice— which is to say it has to be in *her* voice. If *you* say any of this, you are a dead man.

Plan D: Break up.[*] Get the hell outta there. Head for the hills. Tell her it's not working for you. Tell her it's you, not her. Tell her whatever you want, just get out of the relationship and never look back. You'll have to pick the perfect time to do this. Like when her father is away.

I know you kind of like Plan D. You'll even tell your buddies that you've got a good mind to just dump her and move on. That's not true—you don't have a good mind. So chances are you'll put your doubts and fears and courage aside and ask her to spend the rest of her life with you.

IS IT LOVE OR JUST GAS?

One of the toughest problems facing a young man with a raging libido and no acceptable outlet is knowing whether he's in love or just reacting to some baser instinct like lust, greed or hopeless desperation. I answered a letter from a Lodge Member (L.M.) on this subject and am reprinting it here as a way to help you decide whether you're looking for a life partner or just a fun way to fill in thirty-five to forty minutes.

Dear Red,

I have met a new girl at school and I can't get her out
of my mind. I think about her all the time. I walk by her
house three or four times a day hoping to get a glimpse of
her. I've lost my appetite and have trouble sleeping. I'm
hoping one day to get up enough nerve to ask her out or at
least talk to her, but before I get too committed to this

---

[*]   This plan makes you a real man, or a real idiot, or both.

thing, I wanted to ask you if you think I'm in love or am I just weird.

L.M.

Dear L.M.,

No, you're not just weird. You're weird. But you're not *just* weird. It's hard for me to completely evaluate your situation because I don't have enough information, but for starters, the fact that you'd sit down and write me this letter doesn't sound like a person with a very busy schedule. So I would suggest that you could just be looking for a diversion from your boring life of playing video games and writing letters to international television celebrities.

Similarly, when you say, "I think about her all the time," I need to know what you were thinking about prior to meeting her. If you've previously been thinking about cold fusion or genetic biochemistry, that would be more significant than if you're been thinking about quadruple cheese-bacon burgers and Pamela Anderson.

You say you can't get her out of your mind, but that may just be because there's not much else in there. I also question the loss of appetite. You didn't send a picture, so I'm just guessing here, but I would say that if you're under 5'6" and weigh more than 300 pounds, you haven't lost your appetite, you've just worn it out. I'm sure if you let it rest for a while, it will return.

And when you say you're not sleeping, do you mean at night or during class?

I don't have enough of the facts to make a conclusive decision, but that's never stopped me before, so here goes: I would say no, you're not in love. I say that for three reasons:

1) That's the easiest thing for me to say and I don't care.

2) If you're not in love, me saying that will allow you to cut bait and move on. And I'm sure the girl will thank me.

3) (This is the big one.) Even though I say you're not in love and you believe you're not in love, if you in fact *are* in love, nothing you do or say will change that. Some hidden powerful force will make you act on it.

So start focusing on the girl. She would probably enjoy a letter. At least a lot more than us international television celebrities do.

Red Green

LOOK FOR THE SIGNS

I was driving down the highway the other day and I noticed the usual array of traffic signs—speed limit, cattle crossing, etc. And it struck me that most of these signs are not there to *inform* the motorist, they're there to *remind* him of things he already knows. That's because men in particular are easily distracted and need reminders to keep them aware of their environment. It also struck me that the same approach would be helpful in the bedroom. A man is never more distracted than when he's feeling amorous, so some highway signs in the bedroom might greatly improve his performance. Here are a few to start with:

WHY MEN WON'T COMMIT

Now, I'm going to say some things here, and I know some people are going to say, "Well, that's not true because not all men are like that—my George is not like that," and I'm sure he's not, but let me address those concerns while trying to hide my actual reaction, which is extreme apathy. So, okay, maybe not all men are like the following. Maybe not even most men. Maybe not even some men. Maybe it's just me. But that's all I've got and it's gotten me this far, so I'm going to stick with it.

Okay, here's my point: men are hardwired not to commit. If you look at almost every species in nature, the male dominates a herd of females and treats them all pretty much the same, not really committing to any. Oh, I guess a certain bull might prefer a certain cow based on the sexy way she chews her cud or the size of her udder, but it's very unusual. By design, the man's role is mostly superficial and almost unnecessary. Other than the minute and a half of fertilization (or three minutes for those sensitive French bulls), the male is not really a factor in the propagation of most species. So it's only natural that, as men, it's very difficult for us to think about the long term. We look at Grandpa, and if that's long-term thinking, yikes.

Even the toys we choose are for the short term. We're pretty much bored with them as soon as we open the box. Nobody buys a Corvette thinking they'll drive it forever. I know men buy minivans, but I think they're forced to. How many single men buy them?

I also think part of the problem is that men have more trouble dealing with disappointment. Women can take it in their stride. Men, not so much. Disappointment is personal and it hurts. And for men who aren't good at feeling emotions, disappointment may be the only one you get. So after years of watching commercials or sending away cereal box tops or having Ed McMahon tell us we may already have won, it's understandable to see why men avoid opportunities to be let down. When we see a toy or a trip or a woman advertised, we're so gullible we imagine how much fun we're going to have and how great it's going to be and we get wound up. Our parents try to warn us not to get too excited, but it's no use. It's our job to get excited. If men didn't get excited, the human race would have ended fifty thousand years ago. We're programmed to get excited, which also makes us programmed to be disappointed.

And that's why commitment is so hard for us. We really enjoy the excitement part, but that other thing is hard to take. So men need to be coached in that area. Rather than criticize us for being too excited, I think women need to focus on our disappointment and convince us that our eventual disappointment in them will be far less than our disappointment in any other life choice we could make and will absolutely be more pleasant than our disappointment in ourselves.

When it's time to commit, it's also time to decide what you're committing to, and by how much. Be aware that women's liberation created a lot more power for them and a lot more choices for men. Cohabitation was no longer thought of as living in sin. In some rare cases, having a purely physical relationship became acceptable to women. (It had always been acceptable to men.) And with the rise in the divorce rate, there were financial considerations—marrying a divorcée meant her losing her alimony payments, which might be the couple's only income. Also, if you suspect the marriage is not going to go the distance, it's a lot cheaper to not even start the trip.

In my personal view, I prefer being married because it's a legally binding contract, and I didn't think a woman would ever put up with me forever unless the courts got involved. And marriage demands a lot more of you. Being married is like serving a prison term. Living common-law is like being under house arrest.

If you decide to live together, it's obviously less of a commitment but there are even different levels within that arrangement:

Most Committed. Suggest that the two of you find a new home and live there together. This is going to take more time and involves each of you making a life change.

Less Committed. Ask her to move in with you. You make no sacrifices. Your only changes are you've added a free cook and cleaner, with benefits.

Least Committed. Move in with her. You get all of the above, rent-free.

I'm thinking these relationships have to be less stable. I know the divorce rate is up there, but after watching *Judge Judy* for seventeen years, I'd say the living-together thing has an even higher failure rate. So I suggest you man up and do the proposal thing.

But it's tricky. You have to pick the right moment and do it in the right way, and mainly, you have to be absolutely sure that she is going to say yes. Moose T. tells of his unfortunate experience with Cindy M., the star of the Possum Lake intermediate women's softball team. Moose was umpiring the game and had arranged for a Cessna 172 to fly over the stadium when Cindy was up to bat.

It was trailing a banner saying, "Cindy, will you marry me?—Moose." Cindy hit a soaring pop fly that brought the plane, and Moose, down. He revoked the proposal and called her out on the infield fly rule. He forgot to make sure she would say yes.

Stinky P. had the complete opposite experience. He was standing next to his girlfriend when his trick knee let go and he dropped to the ground. He reached up for her hand and said, "Will you carry me?" She burst into tears and said yes. She thought she was marrying him; he thought she was carrying him. Ultimately they were both right.

THE PROPOSAL

One of the best ways to ensure a positive outcome is to keep the whole process very traditional. Start by asking her father's permission—even if you have to do it during prison visiting hours. And stick to the script. Tell him you'd like to ask for his daughter's hand. Don't add that you're also interested in a few other parts.

If you're sure she will say yes and you're sure you want her to, it's still important to choose a suitable moment and setting for popping the question. Here are some conditions that enhance a marriage proposal:

- moonlight
- violin music
- long-stemmed roses
- a promotion
- a lottery win
- a romantic dinner
- a tuxedo
- the correct amount of after shave

Here are some that kill a marriage proposal:

- a bad smell
- accordion music
- your unemployment
- a chainsaw starting
- a Speedo
- a cubic zirconium ring

The proposal is the most difficult thing you'll ever do with your mouth, and that includes eating at an East Indian restaurant. That's because you have to say the right words at the right time in the right place to the right person. I'm betting you've never done that before in your life. We have to assume that you want the woman to say "yes," otherwise you wouldn't be asking, so here are a couple of guidelines to help you get the desired results:

The Right Place

Somewhere reasonably quiet. Not between heats at a monster truck rally. But not too quiet. Not in a library or a funeral home. You need romantic quiet. I suggest a high-end restaurant, and by high-end I don't mean a rooftop Burger King. I'm talking expensive food and great service, with soft lights and music. Don't sit at the bar. Don't sit near the kitchen or the restrooms. Find a secluded, low-traffic area where you two can have some privacy. This is a very personal moment. If she accepts, you can embrace without onlookers. If she declines, you can do that fake laugh without the worry that you're not fooling anyone.

The Right Time

You need her full attention and her best mood. You need her mind to be clear and at rest so she can fully appreciate the unbelievable offer you are making. If she's just had a tough day at work and is about to be incarcerated, you should wait out the three months less a day. If she's upset about her family or her friends or is having a bad hair day, you should probably hang on for a week or so.

Sometimes you can save the situation by putting her in a happy mood before popping the question. Maybe even tell her a joke, but stay away from sewage stories or any jokes that have the word *boobs* in the punchline. Get her to laugh at somebody you both know. Not herself. It's way too early for that.

If you're brave, you can get her to laugh at you, but don't get mad when she has trouble stopping. Instead, get her to laugh at the waiter or somebody else in the restaurant. But not the big guy at the bar with the jagged scar through the middle of his "What are you looking at?" tattoo. The right time to propose is based completely on her mood. It's not always easy to spot the right time, but you'll know immediately if you've picked the wrong time.

The Right Words

There are certain words and phrases that really up your chances of a successful proposal. I suggest *love, together, forever,* "the perfect one for me," *eternity,* "grow old together," "have children," "make you happy" and "you're my whole world."

Conversely there are words and phrases that should be avoided. Things like "give it a try," "you're not gonna do any better," "hump our brains out," *stud,* "shack up," "live in your mom's basement" and "I'll quit my job."

The Right Person

This is a fallacy. People are constantly changing. The right person for you today will not necessarily be the right person for you tomorrow, unless you both change in a way that continually closes the gap. So the right person is the right person not for the way they are when you marry them, but for the way they will adapt to whatever changes the marriage has to go through to survive. Successful marriages are based on equality and fairness. So if the girl you're marrying is a lot more equal and fair than you are, she's a good choice. However, you're the one who'll have to do some changing.

NO MEANS NO

When you ask a girl to marry you and she says no or even "No, thanks," that can make you feel a little awkward. You need to be able to come back with a witty rejoinder of some kind that somehow either breaks the tension or gives her the same kind of surprise you've just experienced. Here are a few sample responses to help you regain your pride after she says no:

- "I'm sorry. I thought you were someone else."
- "Oh, thank God. I thought you were pregnant."
- "I'll tell the football team that you're still available."
- "Do you know any other girls who want to get married?"
- "My mistake. I should have guessed you were gay."
- "Good call. We would have had ugly kids."
- "Well, that saved us both a messy divorce."
- "Great. Who am I going to cheat on now?"
- "No? Oh my God, I came <u>that</u> close to marrying an idiot! And so did you."

PREPARATION FOR HAPPINESS (PREPARATION H)

If, on the other hand, she accepts your proposal of marriage, you will go down a new path in your life. A path like no other you have ever encountered and from which there is no turning back.

Marriage is like the military draft. It changes you forever. Even if you don't see much action. But before you get to the marriage, you've got to go through the preparation for the big day, and, as in the military, it's referred to as the rules of engagement.

Immediately after the accepted proposal and the wearing of the engagement ring, there is a huge burst of relief and euphoria from all of your friends and family, who, up until then, felt there was very little hope for either of you. That celebration will sometimes last as long as an hour. After that, you'll be under pressure to pick a date for the wedding and start making the arrangements.

Your biggest challenge is to not reveal the truth. If you can pull that off, it will help you tremendously once you're married. The truth is, you're in no big hurry to get married. It may have taken you seven years to propose—there's no need to rush now. But don't tell her that. Any delay will cause her to assume your proposal was insincere or that you're having second thoughts or that you're just stringing her along. That can be especially damaging if it's true.

So instead, blame it on your unworthiness to be her husband—you want to wait until you're making more money or have a down payment saved up or win the lottery. You want to be able to give her a great life and would rather wait until you're in a financial position to do so.

But you'll need to project an acceptable timetable. Like you'll be getting a big raise at your pizza delivery job as soon as your driver's licence is reinstated. Or you have a great-aunt on her deathbed who is leaving you a rare collection of Hummel figures and a '76 Pacer. The trick is to be convincing without being specific. If she starts getting antsy, remind her that she used to be one of your girlfriends, and then she became your only girlfriend and now she is your fiancée. Yes, someday soon she will be your wife, but she shouldn't be cheated out of the fiancée experience. Being a fiancée is way more romantic than being a wife. Fiancée is French. Wife is German. I think.

But for the vast majority of men, a date needs to be locked in right away—especially if you're the kind of man who has been known to underdeliver on previous promises.

Picking the date will be very difficult, as the bride wants to ensure good weather and the availability of friends and relatives while you're trying to avoid all of the fishing derbies and the opening of deer season. As the days progress the conflicts will escalate and the number of difficult decisions will grow exponentially. There are times in a man's life when he has to stop the madness, put his foot down and dictate how things are going to unfold. This is not one of those times. Just go along to get along. Any contrary opinion you express during this time will end up coming back and hitting you right in the nuptials.

Your fiancée is already dealing with a lot of difficult people; don't add yourself to that list. Her biggest problem will be her mother, who wants to use your wedding to make up for her disappointment over marrying your future father-in-law. The mother of the bride wants everything to be the absolute best it can be. She'll want to be involved in all the choices. Let her. She wasn't allowed to pick the groom, so cut her some slack.

Despite the four thousand years of jokes to the contrary, you need your mother-in-law to like you. Your wife will find plenty of things about you to criticize—you don't want her mother agreeing with her. So let your mother-in-law have a free hand for the wedding plans. She's focused, she has an agenda and she's paying. When the event finally happens, it may be your *night*, but it's her day.

WHAT'S IN A NAME?

You may find that once you are engaged, your fiancée will give you a nickname of some kind. It will be a term of endearment where the term will most likely be longer than the endearment. Be very particular about the nickname she chooses, because you will have it for a long, long time.

Something short and semi-cool is about the most you can hope for—Honey, Baby, that kind of thing. If it's way too respectful, like Ace or Champ, it usually means the exact opposite of what it says. Also, watch out for the cute ones—Poofy Bear, Lambykins, etc. There's no way your friends will let that go.

Generally limit the nickname to no more than two syllables and ensure it contains at least one hard consonant, and you can't go too far wrong. Probably the safest nickname is a shorter version of your last name—if your last name is Hankmeister, and she calls you Hank, that's fine. However, if your last name is Dorkweiler, you'll want to go another way.

But no matter what nickname you decide on, you need to understand the real reason she wants to give you one in the first place. It's so she can put your real name aside, which allows her to use it against you later. For example, let's say your name is Bob Dungflescher. She's not going to find a nickname there, and if you expect her to take your name when you marry, that could be a deal breaker.

So let's say that even though your name is Bob, she nicknames you Shorty, for reasons known only to the two of you and the sex therapist. From that day forward, as life drifts into its inevitable routine, she will refer to you as Shorty. She is now building up an arsenal of names to call you if things go wrong—including "arsenal." And the most effective names to call you are the ones that are actually versions of your name, Bob. So whenever she calls you something other than Shorty, you'll instantly know something is amiss.

And she will vary the use of those names based on how wrong things are. If you've just done something that's stupid but also mildly amusing—like had an egg explode in the microwave—she will call you Bobby, implying an immature version of yourself. If you've done something stupid and annoying—like had a dozen eggs explode in the car—she will call you Bob, implying you're a man and better get that cleaned up before the dog smells it. If you've done something stupid and dangerous—like had the car explode in the garage—she will call you Robert, implying she sees you as a suspicious stranger who will now have to sleep in the car in the garage even though neither any longer exists.

The other hint you get as to how deep you're in whatever you're in is the tone and volume of the name she calls you. If it's just above normal conversation level, you will survive and get back to life as normal in a relatively short period of time. If it's way louder than that, this is going to take a few days. If it's the loudest thing you've ever heard and just below the frequency that only dogs can hear, you're going to need a fantastic memory to be able to remember what your bedroom looks like.

However, even that is not the ultimate level of displeasure she can demonstrate. When she calls you Robert in a flat, even tone, well below normal conversation level and delivered with a piercing stare from dead eyes, you, my friend, have pinned the needle and will find yourself in solitary confinement, even when she's in the room.

GOING FERAL

When a domesticated animal is abandoned in the wild, it can become *feral,* which means that in order to survive in a harsh environment, it reverts back to a more primitive state. The same thing can happen to you if you live too long on your own before bringing a woman into your home. Here are some signs that you have gone feral and that it may be too late for you to have a normal married life:

- You only shave when there's a full moon.
- When you go to bed, you take off your underwear and toss it onto a lampshade. It is your underwear for this week.
- Your underwear for next week is in the toe of one of your sneakers.
- Your microwave oven, although new, looks like you've used it for a hundred years. Your washer and dryer, on the other hand, are in showroom condition.
- Your car is so full of fast food bags and wrappers, when you go over a bump it rustles.
- You own one suit that your mom bought you for graduation. It has never been cleaned.
- You have not had a date in over three months.
- You have not had a second date since 1987.
- You subscribe to the most expensive TV cable package they offer and you pay extra to have them exclude the Women's Network and the Food Channel.
- You never know the dates of Thanksgiving or Easter but can name the starting time and location of the last twenty-three Super Bowl games.
- You drink beer out of the can.
- You drink wine out of the can.
- You spend a lot of time in the can.
- You fantasize about a blind date with a porn star.
- Nothing anybody ever says or does offends you.
- You can sleep on any surface in any position at any time. Especially at work.
- Here's the main problem: you're not unhappy.

THE IMPORTANCE OF OLD FRIENDS

The difference between committing to a life partner and dating is like the difference between sixty years of car payments and taking test drives for the rest of your life.

Oh sure, with the test drives you get the variety and the excitement of seeing what this baby can do, but for most people a lifetime of shallow dives is not nearly as fulfilling as one deep plunge.

But make no mistake, the goal of a monogamous, happy marriage is extremely elusive and takes a lot of effort and vigilance. You need as much help as you can get. If your parents had a good marriage, that's a bonus. Most people get married in spite of, rather than because of, their parents' experience.

So rather than focusing on your parents, I think it's better to have lifelong friends who are going through the same experiences. People you can relate to. People you can teach and learn from. People who give you a sense of normalcy when you think you're the only person in the world who feels the way you do. But you have to work at keeping those friendships alive and current. You have to make an effort to see those people and be in their lives.

Some of them will seem just like you—going through the same problems and having the same results. They will give you comfort. Some will seem to be doing better than you—they get along better, they look better, they're more successful. They will give you ambition. Some will be doing a lot worse than you—they fight all the time, they look bad and they're facing financial ruin. These are the most important friends because they will give you hope. You want them to succeed because if they do, you'll do even better. But even if they fail and you don't, it will give you the feeling that you have a chance.

In my experience, some of the most successful-looking marriages did a crash and burn and some of the shakiest had a miraculous breakthrough. But the important lessons come from knowing people over a lifetime. There's a shorthand between friends who've known each other a long time and have shared experiences. Oh sure, you'll make new friends throughout your whole life, but it's great if you can keep a special place in your life for your old friends. It's very similar to the decision you made when you got married—you don't want to spend your life test-driving friends, either.

SIGNING UP

People have different ways of looking at the transition from bachelorhood to married life. Some consider it the end of personal freedom and a carefree life. Similar to going through puberty, things start to get way more complicated. Personally, I prefer to think of it as signing up for the military. Like you considered all the options, the performance expectations, the working conditions, the term, and decided to make a commitment for yourself, your family and your country.

And this is not like signing up for the national guard, the light infantry, the navy or even the air force. This is like signing up for the marines. It's going to take *that* level of courage, perseverance and, most of all, discipline to make this mission a success. On the upside, your bride hopefully isn't looking for a few good men, but rather one half-decent man—you. But make no mistake, just like the marines, there are rules, there is a protocol and there most definitely is a code. Sometimes it's just a dress code, but it's a code nonetheless.

On the downside, none of the rules that you must adhere to and live by are written down anywhere. They vary from woman to woman and they vary from day to day with each woman. You are facing a constantly moving target on an ever-changing battlefield. Your greatest assets are your intentions and your patience.

As long as your intentions are to make that woman happy, you will be forgiven almost every shortcoming of your performance on all levels—physical, emotional and intellectual—for the marriage to which you have dedicated your service. And if you're patient, you will have a much better chance of success as you wait until the absolute last minute to decide on a course of action that is therefore much more in sync with the wishes of mission control (your wife).

I wouldn't call it a war, but it certainly is a struggle and, as with all conflicts in life, you will have days when you will lose ground, days when you will gain ground and days when you will *be* ground. Finely ground. But over the long haul, if you are the marine I think you are, you will prevail.

Don't expect rewards in the form of badges of honour or citations from the commander-in-chief. The acknowledgment of your loyalty and dedication will be expressed on a daily—or, more specifically, nightly—basis. But when it's all said and done, when you saw the hill and took the hill and then built a four-bedroom backsplit *on* the hill, you'll be able to look yourself in the eye because you are the few, you are the lucky, you are the proud, and you made it look like you were just following orders.

THE LAUNCH SEQUENCE

Aside from the planning and preparation for the wedding, there is a series of rituals that happen in a specific order. The common fear is that if you miss any of these steps, your marriage will be doomed. However, if you do everything perfectly, the marriage may also be doomed. So you don't really do them for the long-term success of your marriage; you do them for the short-term success of you retaining your position as groom.

Getting the Word Out

You might think that the first layer of people who need to know you're engaged are friends and family. That is not correct. It must be family and friends. If your mother finds out you're engaged from the sister of one of your drinking buddies, you're in trouble. So tell family first, and more specifically, tell your parents first. And don't do it together. You tell your parents and let her do the same. You don't want her to see the look of relief on your parents' faces and she doesn't want you to see the look of disappointment on hers. Once the parents have been told, you can work your way through the family in descending order of the potential value of their wedding gifts.

Next, tell your friends, but do that together. It will hopefully prevent them from saying something insensitive. Chances are your fiancée's parents will want to put an announcement in the local paper. Make sure they use a picture of her alone, just in case anyone in the collection or law enforcement business is looking for you.

It's best to get the news of your engagement out there as quickly as possible. It will limit the timeline of old boyfriends and girlfriends coming out of the woodwork and making claims they can't prove, even though the child looks just like you.

The Wedding Gifts

If you're marrying into a family that thinks it's rude to say, "Just give us cash," you'll have to find creative ways to orchestrate the wedding gifts. You have certain items that you want. However, there are a lot of items you don't want, and sure, you can turn them into quick cash, but you run the risk of the donor seeing them in the window at the pawnshop.

Traditionally, the bride and groom register for gifts at a store they like, and they even identify the specific items they want. You can actually use this registry as a way to get cash gifts by telling guests they have the option of giving cash if they'd prefer and then not registering any gift under $1,000 in price. Sweet.

Ask them to send the wedding gifts well ahead of the day, and imply that the generosity of the gift will affect where they'll be sitting at the reception.

The Bridal Shower

In the last few years there's been a trend to do a thing called a "stag and doe" so that the shower is attended by couples, rather than just women. This pretty much guarantees that nobody will have a good time. The men will have no appropriate jokes to tell and the women will have nothing to talk about.

The old-school all-women shower is the way to go. It's a mix of female family and friends with stories from their widely varied marital experiences, which they use to terrorize the bride. A lot of important intimate secrets and advice are exchanged. That's why it needs to be all women. It's not a party. It's the first official meeting of your wife's support group. In the long run it will create a safety net for her and take the heat off you. I'm thinking you'll need it more than she will.

The Rehearsal

You may think rehearsals are a good thing—especially if you've been lucky enough to have a honeymoon rehearsal—but that will change. The wedding rehearsal is usually a day or two before the wedding, and most of the women there are already stressed out because the flowers haven't arrived yet and the minister has a lisp and the ring bearer has pink eye and one of the bridesmaids is a guy now. And the fact that the men are relaxed and glib only adds to the exacerbation.

So when you're there, focus on the highest authority in the church—the mother of the bride—and do exactly what she tells you, exactly *when* she tells you. Otherwise, Do Not Talk or Move. It will be hard to focus because, as the groom, you have nothing to do. But you need to do it perfectly. So get there early, wait for your orders, execute and then get the hell out of there.

The Stag

Now you're talking. The stag is the last rite of passage as you move away from the carefree world of your buddies into the responsibilities of a married man. And their way of not being forgotten is to make sure you have a hangover that lasts the rest of your life. But it's still a very important component in the process.

The purpose is to give the groom a worthy send-off while reminding him of the great life he's giving up. When done properly, neither one of these happens. The groom is an incoherent wreck at the wedding and his memory of his buddies is gratitude just for having survived. So he's incapable of making decisions and convinced there isn't enough Aspirin in the world to allow him to return to his single life. In both cases, it puts him in the perfect mental state to get married.

The entry in Buster's Diary after his stag:

Deer Dairy,
Jist got hom frum stag. Head sore. Mouth dry. Pants wet.
Going bed.

The Ceremony

Almost nobody has less to do than the groom. There's a reason for that. History has taught us that giving the groom too much to do on a day when he's second-guessing everything is not in anyone's best interest. So your two main functions are to do exactly what the minister tells you to do, and to make your sure your zipper is done up.

Don't worry about anything else. Don't even worry about the minister's zipper. And if the minister's zipper is in fact not done up, don't reach over and fix it, or the bride's mother will faint.

You just walk out a few steps to the altar, with the best man and ushers preventing you from turning back, then you watch your bride come up the aisle. Unless you have a master's in English, do not write your own vows. Nobody wants to hear the word *horny* in church. Just do the standard boilerplate vows, which you will repeat after the minister, and then put on the ring and kiss the bride. And here again, try to keep that kiss G-rated. The kiss is part of the wedding, not part of the honeymoon.

After you leave the church, you have to keep pretending you're enjoying this at least until the photographer is done.

The Reception

In the old days, receptions were very formal and stodgy, but now they tend to be informal and relaxed. This is a huge mistake. Stodge is your friend.

When you get relaxed, you think you're funny and everyone pays the price. Next thing you know, you're toasting the maid of honour by calling her "a real fun girl with a great set of knockers." You're not supposed to say that. You're not supposed to know that. You're not supposed to notice that. Mainly, you're not supposed to care.

Keeping the reception formal is also your best chance of shutting down the other speeches. Like your brother going into great detail about your rap sheet or that time you came home from Lovers' Lane with your pants on backwards.

The point of the wedding reception is for your friends and family to send you off into your married life with the best possible chance of finding happiness. While occasionally speeches are touching and supportive, they have started way more wars than they have ended. And drinking makes it even worse.

Alcohol and public speaking make for an explosive mixture. I suggest you either serve your guests no alcohol or way too much. You want them either sober or incoherent.

Another dangerous modern trend is for the bride and groom to stay at the reception until the bitter end, and it usually is. You have got to get out of there as early as possible. The whole wedding day is a ticking time bomb from the moment your eyes open. You don't want to end the day by getting them opened even more. When the bride and groom drive off, that's a signal to Uncle Bob that maybe that tenth beer is not a good idea. You control how volatile the party gets by how long you ask people to like each other. By the time the reception starts, you're already four or five hours into that challenge—don't push your luck.

If the guests decide to take the party somewhere else or even have a fight in the parking lot, you did what you could, it's not your fault, and you'll still get back your deposit.

The Honeymoon

This is another aspect of the wedding that has changed radically over the years. In the traditional sense, the honeymoon was the consummation of the marriage, where two virgins (one virgin if the other one was the king) would unite physically. It made it a special night and added a tremendous amount of anticipation, even if the reality fell way short of the mark.

These days, many relationships are consummated long before the wedding, in the back seat of an SUV or in the last row of the movie theatre or under the stands at the baseball stadium. On the one hand, it takes the incentive out of the honeymoon, but on the other it avoids any unpleasant surprises arriving too late for either party to easily get out of the relationship.

It's really up to each couple to make the call. In my opinion, sex is great, but it's not worth getting married for.

REGRETS ONLY

No matter how much work and planning you put into your wedding, something is bound to go wrong. Don't let it ruin your day. Just deal with it and move on. In the long run your marriage is much more important than your wedding. If you're looking for a wedding that went worse than yours, check this letter that Stinky and Wanda P. sent to their guests.

Dear Wedding Guests,

Wanda and I would like to thank almost all of you for attending our wedding. It was a beautiful day and nobody died, so overall we think it went well. However, as you may have noticed, there were a few glitches, so we wanted to send you this letter of apology to let you know we were not pleased with everything that happened and to also remind you that wedding gifts are irrevocable.

    I'm sure many of you were as shocked as we were to find out the guy with the messy hair and the Bermuda shorts was in fact the minister. He was a last-minute replacement and had decided that it would put the guests at ease if he had a few snorts for breakfast and told everyone to just call him Bob. As for his choice of scripture, I'm not sure the excerpts about Sodom and Gomorrah were appropriate, and Wanda was particularly offended at the amount of detail Reverend Bob provided concerning the level of debauchery that existed in those two towns. As it turns out, many of Bob's stories were not from the Bible but rather from his own personal experience as a goat herder.

    Wanda also asked me to express her regret over what we're now calling the wedding dress "malfunction." Wanda bought the dress almost a year ahead of the wedding day and she had every intention of getting down to a size 8 by then. And I think we all could see she was well on her way, but only made it down to a 24. Since the dress could not be returned and we could not postpone the wedding without losing our deposit on the Legion, Wanda decided—with the help of four jars of Vaseline and a couple of warm spatulas—to put the dress on. She said she had never been that uncomfortable in her life and I know when you saw her, you shared that feeling. Some of the teenage boys in attendance were trying to identify the various body parts sticking out of the dress and, as the groom, I can assure you that you were all wrong. But then I'm sure you realized that when the dress gave way during the ceremony. I feel I am partially to blame as I didn't realize that wearing an extremely tight dress could increase the diameter of a person's ring finger, and I probably should just have handed her the ring rather than try to force it on there. Ultimately, it was my rapid jerking up and down of her arm that caused the dress to rip, or rather explode. Wanda also wanted me to point out that her lack of underwear was not a flirtation—it was to make her smaller. I know it was an especially traumatic moment for Old Man Sedgwick, who was sitting in the front row. They tell me he's starting to recognize voices and will eventually regain his sight.

As for the wedding reception, the one lesson we all came away with is that it's good to have insurance. And next time we will. For any of you who are getting married in the future, I would suggest you don't have an open mic. People have no sense of decorum. I don't understand how an invited guest would use that as an opportunity to tell the world about the money you owe them. Guests are supposed to be classy, courteous and patient. Not clinking incessantly on your glasses and forcing me to kiss Wanda while she still had a mouthful of mashed potatoes.

And for the bridal flower toss, I want to make it clear that it was Wanda's enviro-dork sister who insisted that the bouquet be made entirely of nectarines. And maybe if Buster Hadfield had been paying attention, he would have seen it coming and it wouldn't have bounced off his head and knocked the candelabra into the cash bar. I'm not sure why we needed that many bottles of vodka, but man, does it burn. Usually, when you describe a wedding reception by saying, "We blew the roof off," it's just a figure of speech.

In closing, let me thank you again for attending and please accept our apologies and, in the interests of all of us getting along in this wonderful community of family and friends, we sincerely ask you to drop all the charges.

As your friend and co-resident, I remain,

Stinky

THE HONEYMOON'S OVER

Most guys don't look too far ahead, which is why they find life so full of surprises. And one of the biggest of those surprises happens after the honeymoon, when you and your wife try to settle into a normal life.

Without thinking about it or verbalizing it, you are expecting that your married life will be just like your single life, except you'll have a helper. Unfortunately, your wife feels the same way. More unfortunately, she's right and you're wrong.

Junior S. told me it was a huge adjustment for him. He didn't expect his life to change much. Oh sure, he was fine with no more cold pizza, no more wearing the same shirt four days in a row, no more lonely nights, but otherwise he was expecting business as usual—empty beer cans on the fridge, empty underwear on the dresser, twenty-four-hour sports channel, shave every other weekend. No. Not even close.

What Junior discovered is that his wife had no intention of allowing him to continue any part of his single life. And Junior wisely realized that his challenge was to accept how horrible that single life had been. He may have enjoyed certain parts of it, and he may, deep down in his heart of hearts, miss the freedom and the lack of decorum and personal hygiene that were the hallmarks of that lifestyle, but for the sake of the marriage, he knew he had to reject any vestige of the life he had before the marriage.

Because for true love to last, each party must believe they have no other viable options. Junior also says it's not enough to just pretend you feel that way. You have to absolutely convince yourself that marriage is the greatest thing that ever happened to you, even when you have lost yourself—when you're wearing clothes you never thought you'd wear and hanging out with couples you don't even like and thinking hard about everything before you say it.

This is not a bad thing for you. The hardest pill for a man to swallow is that, even though she married you, she still felt there was room for improvement. She didn't say "I do" because she thought you were the perfect man. It was more like a football scout watching a high school athlete. They see potential, but it's going to take a lot of practice and coaching for you to be a franchise player. That's her job. She knows what she wants and her mother has taught her how to get it.

Over the next several years, with hard work and coaching, you'll continue to improve and the shared experience will cause your father-in-law to become one of your best friends.

HOWDY, NEIGHBOUR

After you get married, and if it's not feasible for the two of you to live with her parents for whatever reason, you're going to have to go out and get your own place. It may be an apartment, or a small house or a campsite. But whatever it is, you need to sit down with your wife and have a discussion about how to approach your new neighbours.

The basic problem is that your wife is a nice person. She assumes the best in people and is friendly and open with everyone she meets. This is a fine attitude when you're a greeter at Walmart, but it doesn't work well when you're the new person in the neighbourhood. The difference is the customers at Walmart don't know where you live. Even if they really like you and would like to spend more time with you, they have no idea where to find you. Their only hope is to just keep coming back to Walmart. And they do.

Your new neighbours, on the other hand, know exactly where you live and have a pretty good sense of when you're there and when you're not there. So you and your wife need to come to an agreement as to how many of these neighbours you're going to make friends with, and how you're going to decide which ones those are.

It's not unlike the system you used to find each other. You stand back and observe a fairly large sample of people and then, through a process of elimination, you whittle that group down to the chosen few. So for the first few weeks, avoid eye contact and conversation with all of the neighbours. When you get home, just rush right by them into your home, close the door and lock it. If you feel like you're being rude, you can yell something about diarrhea over your shoulder as you go by. Once you're inside, pull a chair up to the edge of the drawn curtains and just observe your neighbours for a few hours.

You'll be amazed at what you can discover just by watching people interact with each other. Have your wife join you so you can discuss what you see. A stepladder makes an excellent vantage point, with one of you sitting on the top and the other one about halfway up.

Remember: the objective is to rule out any neighbours who could be a nuisance once you get to know them. For example, the guy who sits out in front of his building and stares at a tree. You probably don't want him dropping over on a regular basis.

Sometimes you can tell by just looking at their property. The guy with the perfectly groomed house and manicured yard and spotlessly clean car is not the guy you want to hang around with. He clearly has radically different standards from you in terms of how much time you're prepared to devote to keeping a house looking nice. In a matter of weeks he'll be asking you why your place is such a dump.

Then there's the quiet guy on the corner who wears camo and has a gun collection. Don't make him your friend. Don't make him your enemy, either.

But the most dangerous neighbours of all are the friendliest ones. The ones who come running over to welcome you to the neighbourhood and tell you everything about everyone and are so pleasant you want to nail them with the pie they just handed you. The clue here is that they're being overly nice to you and they don't even know you. That's not a compliment, it's a personality disorder. You want people to like you for being *you*, not just for being *there*.

This kind of person is probably lonely, and will infiltrate and then dominate your life. You'd have to be very aggressive to get rid of them. Better to just nip it in the bud.

The neighbours you want are the quiet, reserved couple who pretty much keep to themselves. An occasional wave. If they see you struggling with a load of groceries, they ask if you'd like a hand, rather than just pitching in and maybe seeing some medication you'd rather keep a secret. These are the kinds of neighbours you want. They're there when you need them, but they're not there when you don't.

Try to get your wife to see that people have a lifetime limit of a hundred interactions. If your neighbour drops by once every twelve months, you can last a hundred years before you've had enough. If they drop over twice a week, a year from now you'll be moving. And if that keeps happening, you will eventually become a guy in a camo suit with a gun collection.

STOP DOING THAT

Most single men live in a dream world where they imagine they will find a life partner who will represent an unqualified addition to their lives. They think they'll be allowed to carry on with all of the activities and attitudes they had before they met her. The only difference is that now they'll have a beautiful woman to share their home and their bed and their lives and their bed.

I suppose this may have occurred way back in history before women got the vote or learned how to operate a firearm, but in today's society it is unreasonable for any man not to expect to have to make lifestyle changes to accommodate the wishes of his partner. And I suggest the best way is for you to anticipate those changes and make them on your own, rather than force her to make a federal case out of everything you say and do.

To get you started thinking along those lines, here is a list of activities you should voluntarily give up in the interest of being a responsible husband:

- going to strip clubs
- performing at strip clubs
- picking up female hitchhikers
- coaching the cheerleader team
- participating in, or even winning, pickled egg-eating contests
- exploring Antarctica
- wearing velour
- doing things with your mouth that your male friends find funny

- heli-skiing
- sleeping in your street clothes
- being on the street in your pyjamas
- always thinking about sex
- never thinking about sex
- spending more than one weekend a year with your buddies
- lying around your house
- lying around your yard
- lying around your cell
- forgetting your wife's birthday
- remembering your old girlfriend's birthday
- speaking before thinking
- speaking before sobering up
- speaking before your lawyer is present
- thinking you know everything
- thinking you know enough
- thinking you know anything

THE WIN-WIN OF A MAN CAVE

In the last few years there has been an official recognition of the "man cave." This is an area of the house that has become the designated territory for the man of the house. It's usually in the garage or the basement, but never both. Now, you might think there's an inequality for the man to have his own space while the woman gets none, but the reality is that, over time in a marriage, every other space in the home is the woman's. You can't just leave your shoes on the stove or your underwear on the La-Z-Boy. And just try giving the lawn mower a ring job on the dining-room table.

So after years of bickering about what belongs where, the husband and wife will arrive at a truce. He can have his own space in some remote area of the home, provided that none of his projects or pastimes ever show up in any other area. He gets 5 per cent of the house that's all his, while the other 95 per cent of the house is 85 per cent hers. And because men would rather have all of *something* than part of anything, we call that a win-win.

Personally, I highly recommend a man cave, especially in the garage where a guy's buddies can come and go without ever setting foot in the restricted area (the house). I'm including a preliminary list of furnishings to help get you off on the right foot:

Beer fridge

Backup beer fridge

Tall-boy tool caddy

Workbench with vise (nutcracker)

Exhaust hose for gas motors

Exhaust fan for guests

Oil filter air freshener

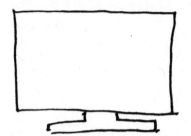

Pirate satellite receiver with continuous code upgrading

86-inch flat-screen high-definition TV (gotta love those big garage doors)

Movie collection   Book collection

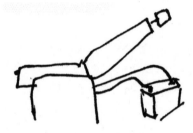

Repurposed reclining front seat from that late-model rental Lexus you totalled (heated, cooled, massage with remote)

Bottle-cap collection (old-school)

Bottle-cap collection (twist-offs)

Theatre-style
popcorn maker

Coffee pot
full of melted
butter

Cheese fridge

Five-gallon deep
fryer full of melted
butter

Sausage fridge

1,000-foot roll
of beef jerky

Telephone with pizza
delivery number on
speed dial

Defibrillator

Johnny-on-
the-Spot

The spot—a.k.a.,
floor drain

A BRAVE NEW WORLD

You're going to have to make a bunch of adjustments once you get married and/or start living together. You probably know each other well enough to have a sense of the big things in your lives, like what kind of homes and food and social events you enjoy. But it's the mountain of little things that will come as the biggest shock. What you wear to bed when it's not a date. How often you eat over the sink. The timetable of clothing that goes from being worn to lying on the floor, to being in the laundry hamper, to being washed, to being ironed, to being put away, to being worn again. That could be years.

But of all of these adjustments you each have to make, nothing is more staggering than what is about to happen to your bathroom. You've always kept it pretty simple: shaving stuff, soap, shampoo, toothpaste and deodorant. Those days are gone. You're about to see more tubes, jars, bottles and spray cans than they have at Home Depot during bug season. The makeup containers alone will represent more shades than the paint department at Psychedelic Warehouse.

There'll be lotions and potions for every situation under the sun. And some for under the moon. There'll be secret formulas to make things look darker or lighter, thinner or fatter, bigger or smaller, younger or older—no, wait, nothing to make things look older; that's what the mirror's for.

There'll be one drawer just for the applicators—short hairbrushes, long-bristle whisks, foam-rubber dabbers, cotton balls, Q-Tips, clay pencils and sandpaper.

You might want to think about beefing up the door on the bathroom cupboard, because you're now going to have a selection of toxic and volatile chemicals in there—hydrogen peroxide, ammonium sulphate, calcium carbonate, etc. If you can find a used particle accelerator on eBay, you could probably make your own nuclear weapon.

Don't even think about questioning what these chemicals do and why there are so many of them. Just trust that your wife is convinced that this science lab is an integral part of her ongoing happiness, and that is all you need to know.

And get ready for the appliances strewn all over the bathroom counters, hanging on the walls and draped over the doorknobs. Hair dryers and curlers and foot massagers and electrolysis guns and laser hair removers and steam facial misters. You may have to rewire the bathroom to have enough outlets. Maybe you should reroute the stove wiring so you can bring 220 volts in there. Just don't put the outlet too close to the bathtub.

And before you get your shorts in a knot and are about to say something insensitive to your wife about what's happened to your bathroom, just stop and think about your garage. Think about the six-foot-high mechanic's tool chest overflowing with every kind of hand tool on the market. And all the power tools hanging on the walls. Not to mention the Shop-Vac, air compressor and hydraulic lift lying on the garage floor. And why do you need all that? To work on your car. Your baby. Well, your wife has all her tools to work on her body, which is *her* baby. The bathroom is now her garage. Just accept it and move on.

However, this does not mean that the garage is now your bathroom.

THE PATH OF LEAST RESISTANCE

For centuries, women have accused men of always wanting to take the path of least resistance. Now, I know a lot of you like things to be black and white, absolute, yes or no, guilty or not guilty. Well, sorry, but I'm going to plead "guilty with an explanation."

And here's the explanation. Let's begin by examining the premise of "path of least resistance." How did that get a negative connotation? What is so offensive about taking the path of least resistance?

Let's say I have an errand to run. To the beer store. And there are two ways I can go. I can glide south downhill for a mile and a half and approach the store from the east, which is the side the drive-thru is on, *or* I can go due north over a glacial mountain for 134 miles and then approach the store from the west. So I'm thinking I'll take the downhill glide and be home in ten minutes.

Now, I know many of you are appalled. "Oh my word, he took the path of least resistance." Yes. I also took the path of least stupidity. So let's admit that the path of least resistance almost always makes the most sense.

Next, let's look at the lives of most men. Men are generally not as intuitive or as sensitive as women, so they don't usually anticipate the world's reactions to their projects or ideas nearly as well as women do. Consequently, they get more unpleasant surprises, on average, than women get. Men generally behave in a way that women expect. Women generally behave in a way that completely baffles men.

What I'm saying here is that in their professional lives, as well as in their personal lives, men are constantly bombarded with surprisingly negative reactions to their ideas and proposals and, by inference, to themselves as people.

Let's take a closer look at that phrase "negative reactions." Is there perhaps a word that says the same thing? Yes, I believe there is. And I believe that word is *resistance*. If you get a negative reaction from someone, they are trying to thwart you. And thwarting, even in its mildest form, is resistance. So what I'm telling you is that men, because of their inherent lack of sensibility and through no fault of their own, experience resistance all the time in every aspect of their professional and personal lives.

And after a few years of that, they're tired of the fight. They're confused. They need a hug. Failing that, when they see the path of least resistance, it's like an oasis to them. A respite from the rejection that permeates everything they try to do. Sure, they take the path of least resistance. What did you expect? Did you think they would take the path of *most* resistance? Even men aren't that crazy.

ONE BED TOO MANY

I know there are married couples out there who, for one reason or another, have separate beds. Maybe one of them often dreams they're a field-goal kicker in the NFL and in their sleep will attempt to put a sixty-yarder through their partner's uprights. Maybe one of them has the habit of clenching the covers with their entire body and then rolling up like a hydraulic cylinder, leaving their partner to swing in the wind of the ceiling fan. Maybe they just don't like anybody touching them when they're asleep. Or awake.

Now, we all know it's not proper to judge other people, but sometimes you have to. Personally, I don't want to live in a world where my wife sleeps in another bed. She might give you a different story, but hey, this is *my* book.

To me, there is nowhere in the world more sacred or personal than my bed. As far as I'm concerned, there's my bed, and then there's the rest of the world. That's how separate it is from any other location. And I'm pretty fussy about who I let into that bed. You're not going to find any of my buddies or the mailman or even that cute little crossing guard in there. It's a very exclusive club. My wife and I are the only members. That suits me fine.

I don't understand why anybody wouldn't want their wife in there with them. I've been in bed alone many times and nothing interesting has ever happened. I'd rather have my wife in there feeling sick than for me to be alone, feeling healthy. Part of the whole appeal of getting married in the first place is to have that place to go together at the end of every day.

My experience with life is that you never know when an opportunity is going to present itself. And when it does, you need to be in the right place at the right time. Being in a different bed is not the right place at *any* time. Women like spontaneity. Not some planned thing. When the two of you are in bed together, you can be spontaneous. You can't do that in separate beds. What do you do if you're suddenly feeling amorous—yell over to her? Or call her on her cellphone? Or wait until she gets up for a glass of water and when she comes back to her bed, you're in it? How gauche.

Now, I'm not saying there's a nightly romp going on in the shared bed. But there could be. And for most men the idea of "could be" is often more exciting than "is." You don't have to shout when you're in the same bed; you can whisper. And if she can't hear you, she can move closer. Then, when she does hear you, she'll move farther away.

But the whole idea of marriage is to allow your partner into your world. That's got to include your bed. And don't tell me you're too big to share a bed. Nobody's too big. Sometimes beds are too small. Get yourself a king-size. Don't worry about the cost; it'll pay for itself in no time because you'll be able to turn the furnace down while simultaneously turning the heat up.

MONEY, MONEY, MONEY

One of the reasons marriage is so tough is because it's not just two people falling in love, it's also a business merger. They are pledging to pool their assets as part of the deal.

This can be a problem. When companies merge, there's a legal responsibility for each party to give full disclosure. Love waives that obligation. So it may not be until after you're married that your wife, who has no debt and a few thousand dollars in the bank, finds out you have less than a hundred bucks and still owe fifteen grand on a car you totalled three years ago. I say you're better off telling her about that long before the wedding. Chances are her dad is running a credit check on you anyway, so it's better if she hears it from you.

They say that money problems can break up a marriage, but those problems always have one thing in common: one of the partners bought something without talking it over with the other. And men are the biggest culprits. That's because we don't like to talk things over. When we talk things over, the point we're trying to make can sometimes sound incredibly stupid. That's because it often *is* incredibly stupid. But here's the problem with being a man: you know it's stupid, *but you want to do it anyway.*

It's actually worse than that. One of the main reasons you want to do it is *because* it's stupid. So people shouldn't say it's stupid—that just encourages us. And I know buying stupid things, like a Russian helicopter or a llama farm, makes for great stories to tell your buddies, but you have one *über*-buddy at this point, and trust me, she will not find those stories amusing.

So it's very important for the financial stability of a couple that only one of you is in charge of the money. It's an easy call if you just look at the two resumés. The one with the better credit rating and positive net worth is a better choice than the one with the maxed-out credit cards and pending litigation. If your wife is the better choice, be man enough to admit it and let her run the finances. If she really loves you, she will occasionally let you do something stupid just so you don't lose your self-esteem.

HOW TO GET TENURE

When university profs have held their teaching jobs long enough that people start to forget they're there, they are awarded a thing called *tenure.* It basically means they can't be fired. In a country that has no royalty, that's as close to being crowned king as you're going to get. This is a great thing. It almost makes up for being a university prof.

As a husband, this is a position you want to strive for. You want to have tenure. You want to know that whatever you do or say, you will not be forced to live in your car. It's a lofty goal, perhaps unattainable, but it's what dreams are made of.

A friend of mine theorized that every time a man does something pleasing for his significant other, like bringing her flowers or doing the laundry or grooming the cat, he is subconsciously awarded one point in her mind. And every time he does something wrong, like getting home late or commenting negatively on her hairdo or doing a face plant into the rum punch, he is penalized ten thousand points.

So getting tenure is a rough go. But it's worth it. If you think you've got what it takes, here's my advice for how you, too (or perhaps I should just say "you") can gain tenure:

> **Be nice.** Don't look for negative things to say. When your wife is upset about her weight gain, don't somehow try to connect that to your hernia. Instead, comment on her beautiful eyes.
>
> **Be thoughtful.** Just for a moment, imagine yourself being a vibrant, attractive, exciting woman who, through circumstances beyond her control, ended up married to you. How would you feel about that? That should make you feel appreciative. Share that feeling.
>
> **Be consistent.** Consider yourself the anchor of the relationship. Not in the sense of holding her back, but in the sense of being grounded and reliable. You need to react to the same stimulus the same way—day in, day out. You know what happens to you when you eat onions? Well, it's kind of like that. Women are reassured by a man who holds his ground.
>
> **Be there.** This is the big one. Men's normal reaction to problems is to either punch somebody or to get the hell outta there.

Neither of those will work. You gotta just hang in. Good news is coming someday, but you gotta be there to get it.

Be her best option. From my limited experience, the best way to get tenure is to convince your wife that you are her best option. And the only way to do that is to let her know that she is *your* best option. I know it's scary, but the best way to get tenure from your wife is to give it to her first.

I'VE GOT A SECRET

They say you should never have secrets from your wife. Well, I'm here to tell you they are dead wrong. If you're in it for the long haul, it's crucial that you have secret information that you've kept from your wife. The more secrets, the better. Not horrible, dark secrets like you once killed a guy with an egg whisk. But rather impressive surprises, like that Nobel Prize you had never mentioned. And I'll tell you why: because that's my style.

You've heard the expression "First impressions are lasting." That's because the only time you really look closely at a person is when you first meet them. At that first encounter, they have all of the attention of all of your senses. You're trying to evaluate their abilities, their IQ, their appearance and intentions.

With each successive meeting, your degree of scrutiny decreases. Eventually, you get to the point where you don't notice anything about them. You've seen it all and heard it all; you've moved on to other projects. A couple who've been married more than twenty years can barely pick each other out of a lineup. That's because humans are weird. We think we want things to stay the same, and when they do, we ignore them. It's as if the key to happiness is to have absolutely nothing in your life that you pay any attention to.

And yet, almost nothing stays the same. So we're constantly on guard, monitoring the changes and trying to figure out how bad things are going to get now.

Over time, you are only interested in the things that change, even though you think you want them to stay the same. This is one of the great mysteries of life, as is non-alcoholic beer. So if you're holding a pen or a crayon or even a grasshopper's butt, you might want to underline this next statement: to keep a relationship alive, you need to continue to find the other person interesting.

That's it. Being attractive is nice. Being athletic is good. Being smart is swell. Being kind is essential. But being *interesting* is the key. And to be interesting you have to say and do things that your partner finds pleasantly surprising.

Sure, you can come home with flowers and candy, but even that becomes a routine after a while. To be truly interesting you need to come up with something new. A new opinion or a new career or a new haircut. You gotta give her something. And when you're stuck, when you've done everything you could think of, when you're at the brink of not being interesting and sliding into the "boring" category where you will sit with almost everybody else she knows, that's when you need to pull out a great secret. Like the time you jumped out of an airplane or shared a cab with Engelbert Humperdinck.

Don't tell her that stuff in the early years. She's got enough to absorb. Wait until you've lulled her into thinking she knows everything about you. And then nail her with a secret. You'll be in for a very romantic night. But keep that a secret too.

SOCIAL TRAPS

You've been married for a while now and things seem to be panning out pretty well. Don't get complacent. Being a married man is a lifelong educational process, and by the time you get your diploma, you'll need bifocals to read it.

You may think you have figured out how to interact socially with your wife, and maybe you have, for certain situations. But what you need to realize is that almost every different social encounter requires a different approach to that interaction. These are called *social traps,* and although they are not traps that are purposely set by your wife, they have the same result—i.e., you get caught and punished.

All of these events can be put into one of four categories, based on the circumstances that led you and your wife to be in the same place at the same time and the relationship of the other people at the event to you and/or your wife. The categories look like this:

Planned Event with Friends and/or Relatives

These are the easiest. Everybody there already knows both of you well enough to have no expectation of you treating your wife better or worse than you ever do. It might be a birthday party or a tailgate party or just the gang getting together to celebrate a case being dismissed. You're off the hook with these folks because the fact they invited you shows they acknowledge you as someone they like, or at least tolerate. You have to really misbehave to get your wife mad at you in this environment. But it's not impossible, which you have proven a few times.

Unplanned Event with Friends and/or Relatives

This is a social encounter that just happens when you accidentally bump into people you know. It could be at the park or the county fair or the mall or the holding area for impounded cars.

This is still one of the easier environments for you to interact appropriately with your wife without her being overly sensitive to the scrutiny of others. However, because it's unplanned, there will be other people there. People you and your wife don't know. People who may not find your chicken dance as entertaining as you do. And your wife will be much more aware of their discomfort in watching you, especially that part where you pretend to lay a very large, untapered egg.

And because she is your wife, she will feel that the criticism is also directed at *her,* which she will feel is unfair and which she will deal with by adding criticism of her own and sending it all your way.

Planned Event With Strangers

This one's trouble. In most cases it's a business get-together, which is bad enough, but when it's your wife's business get-together, it's deadly. Suddenly you're thrust into a group of your wife's co-workers and customers, which is the last place on earth you want to be, and your wife is on high alert that you are going to somehow blow her professional image, which she spent the last four years establishing. And yet she needs you to be there because everybody else is dragging their spouse along and she doesn't want to be the odd one out.

This is not a social event; this is a trap. There is almost no chance of you saying or doing something that your wife's boss or customers will find interesting or amusing. You must, at all cost, avoid talking to these people. And yet, you have to be supportive of your wife. The best approach is to find out if any other woman from the company is at the affair. Ask your wife to introduce you to her, because that way you'll be able to meet her husband. He's your way out. You go to a quiet corner and talk to him for the whole night about cars or motorcycles or even hybrids if you have to. If he only wants to talk about things you find boring, just suck it up and keep the conversation going. You're way better off to be bored with him than to be embarrassing in front of the people who matter.

From a distance, keep an eye on your wife, and every half hour, go over to her, get introduced to whoever she's talking to, be polite, don't make a joke out of any of their facial features, and then offer to get your wife another glass of wine or a canapé. If you're not comfortable saying the word *canapé,* just say "one of those little cheese things that smell kind of funny." The trick is to be attentive, but not too often and never for very long.

Unplanned Event with Strangers

This is the big one. The ultimate test. You're walking down the street and you see your wife having lunch with other women at a sidewalk café. My first warning is: never assume she didn't see you. Wives can see things they weren't even there for. Just accept that you have no chance of getting away. Instead, take a moment and evaluate who she's with. If one of the women is recently divorced, make sure you kiss your wife hello. Otherwise she'll get an earful about how your marriage is in trouble.

At least one of the ladies will invite you to join them. Do not, under any circumstances, accept. They don't really want you to be there, and you feel the same way. If you sit down with these women, that will be the end of all interesting conversation. They're just being polite. You must also be polite by returning the favour and declining the offer. Make up an excuse about a prior commitment you have. But don't use the term "penis enlargement." They don't want to hear the word *penis* and you don't want to say the word *enlargement.*

Be brief. Treat the encounter like a proctology examination— get in and get out as quickly as possible. Be gracious with the ladies and say goodbye to your wife in a way that implies you're looking forward to seeing her later.

Social encounters are much tougher on a marriage than the two of you sitting at home in your underwear watching *Wheel of*

Fortune. You've got to take all of these events very seriously. If you're casual, you will be a casualty.

THE DISENCHANTED FOREST

M ost guys are in a pretty good mood most of the time. They don't fixate on their problems. They don't whine. They're just easy-going, happy guys. It makes them popular and great salesmen.

Unfortunately, it doesn't make them great husbands. That's because most happy guys aren't happy because everything's great; they're happy because they're oblivious to the things that aren't great. Their wives don't usually share that ability to live in Fantasyland, and that creates a rift between them, because when you have a problem, there's nothing more annoying than someone in a good mood.

So as a married man, the first thing you have to watch for are the signs that trouble is brewing. Look for extremes in her behaviour; maybe she is way too loud, or way too quiet. Look for her reactions to your conversation. Does she not even crack a smile at your best joke? Does she laugh long and hard at something you said that wasn't even funny? If so, she's not laughing with you, she's laughing in spite of you.

The secret to a happy life is to be married to a woman who's always in a slightly better mood than you are. You really need to establish that while you're dating because it's hard to change later. I know a few men who tried for most of their lives to get their wives into better moods than theirs, but eventually gave up and became more depressed and miserable than their wives. Mission accomplished.

LAUNDRY THE MANLY WAY

The quickest way to strengthen your relationship is to let your wife know that you appreciate everything she does and that you see the marriage as a partnership where you share responsibilities as often as possible. And that has to include housework.

It's not her job to keep the house clean and tidy while you languish in a universe where salt and fat are the planets and your recliner is the sun. You've got to pull your own weight, and that could be significant.

Now, it's probably safer for everybody if you stay out of the kitchen, but taking over the laundry duties, when done the right way, will be a boon to her and fun for you. But I know that sounds wussy to you, so you need to make a few changes. The first problem is the look of the washer and dryer themselves.

They're usually glossy white, with a splash of chrome. They're designer chic, and designer chic is closer to being a woman than you ever want to get. So for starters, paint the machines flat black and cover the chrome with camo duct tape. *Now* they're looking tough. Add a few racing stickers—Pennzoil or STP or Nitro. You can even throw on a couple of racing stripes if you tend to do small, quick loads. Cover the round dryer door with an imitation mag wheel in polished aluminum and add a couple of Indy-style quick-release hood pins for the top-loading washer door.

Now the machines are starting to look edgy. Throw on some ultraviolet ground-effects lights around the bottom edges and your laundry room is going to look like a biker bar. But as every motorhead knows, looks are not enough. You've got to deliver under the hood. So open up the washer and remove the agitator. Replace it with a Volvo Penta Duoprop marine outdrive circa 1982.

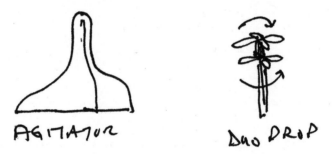

These two racing props delivering opposite rotation are going to beat the crap out of any piece of clothing you throw at them. If you're washing delicates, set the motor speed to "Trolling."

But anybody who does laundry will tell you the real thief of time is the dryer. Not anymore. Pull that baby apart and you'll find a small electric motor running a long, circular belt that goes all the way around the dryer drum, giving you one level of torque and one speed. That's not good enough.

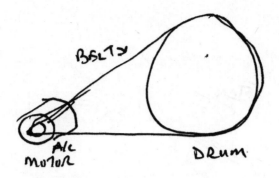

Sure, you need a lot of torque to get it started, but once she's rolling, wouldn't it be great to have another gear to go to? Yes. Yes it would. So throw away the cheesy AC motor and replace it with an AC-to-DC transformer hooked into a golf-cart motor. Now you attach the motor to the driveshaft of a transmission from a mid-'60s British car—Austin, Vauxhall, Morris Minor or similar. Anything that has a four-speed box plus overdrive, connected through a hydraulic clutch.

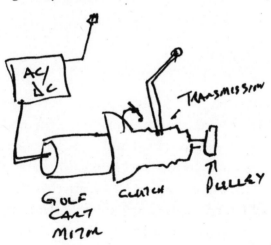

This will allow you to switch gears as the dryer revs up, and eventually max out in overdrive at around 100,000 rpm.

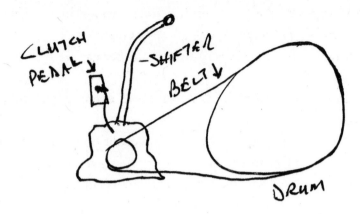

The concept is that spinning the water out of the clothes is faster and more energy-efficient than trying to bake it out. Just be sure to attach the mounting bolts of the dryer directly to the foundation of your home. And do not open the dryer door for at least an hour and a half after the spin cycle.

PRIORITY QUIZ

One of the driving forces behind people's behaviour is the emotional component. For example, they may understand the importance of eating good food and exercising regularly, but if deep down inside they really don't care much about those things, they will not continue to do them. This pattern is exaggerated in a marital relationship because there are only two people involved and because it plays out over such a long period of time.

Finding common ground in what a couple cares about is crucial to them having a successful marriage. Moose T. and his wife, Mrs. T., have been having problems, so we got them to take this Priority Quiz in two separate rooms without being able to consult each other. Here are the results.

1) List, in order, the three most important things in your life.

    MRS. T.: My nails, my cat, Nancy Grace.

    MOOSE: My car, my toolbox, my other car.

2) Can you describe the last romantic evening you had together?

    MRS. T.: It was last summer. We sat out on the porch and just talked about things. We stayed up past midnight. Moose had eaten a bad taco and was afraid to lie down.

    MOOSE: Nope.

3) To celebrate your anniversary, would you like to go to a nice restaurant?

    MRS. T.: Sure.

    MOOSE: When is it?

4) What was it about your spouse that attracted you in the first place?

    MRS. T.: The other guys were worse than him. And he was kind of big and fat, so I knew he could probably get food. Getting him to share it was another hurdle.

    MOOSE: Getting married was just something you did back in the day. If you proposed to a girl and she said yes, you married her. Or if you dated a girl and she said yes, you proposed to her.

5) Looking back over your marriage, do you have any regrets?

    MRS. T.: Yes.

    MOOSE: I don't operate that way. Oh sure, maybe I could have shacked up with some hot-looking babe, but that's all water under the bridge. You learn to move on.

6) How often do you tell your spouse that you love them?

MRS. T.: On New Year's Eve. And it takes a few martinis.

MOOSE: It's implied.

7) If you were trapped on a desert island, who would you want to have there with you?

MRS. T.: My manicurist, my hairdresser and David Hasselhoff.

MOOSE: Nobody.

8) Name your three greatest heroes.

MRS. T.: Nelson Mandela, Walt Disney and Roseanne Barr.

MOOSE: Colonel Sanders, Hugh Hefner and Spider-Man.

9) If you won the lottery, what would you do with the money?

MRS. T.: I'd give some to charity and spend the rest on lottery tickets.

MOOSE: I'd buy a big house for my wife. And I'd live close by.

10) Would you be willing to work with a counsellor to help you make your marriage happier?

MRS. T.: I'd have to think about that.

MOOSE: We don't want to be happier.

Conclusion: Their marriage is fine.

THE GOOD, THE BAD AND THE PORNO

I've never been a big fan of porno movies, but the adult video stores never seem to go out of business, so they must have customers. And I suppose there are some good things about them.

Like you can miss the first twenty minutes or so and still pick up the storyline. And they always have a happy ending.

The performers are generally in excellent physical condition and, although they're not really celebrities, some of the men are certainly larger than life.

But I think overall the negatives far outweigh the positives. These are not classic romances. Not nearly as much resemblance to *An Affair to Remember* as there is to rutting season at the zoo. And I think porno movies provide attitudes and images that are damaging to a normal, healthy relationship between a man and a woman. Here are some reasons for you to not watch them:

- You will start thinking of it as "getting it on" rather than "making love."
- You will expect women to have voracious sexual appetites.
- You will think your mere presence is an irresistible aphrodisiac.
- You will spend most of every weekend shaving.
- You will buy a tanning bed.
- You will think it's okay to have sex with your socks on.
- You will feel like a failure if the session takes way less than an hour.
- You will feel like a failure if the session takes way <u>more</u> than an hour.
- You will increase your expectations while simultaneously reducing your chances.
- You will think it's normal to have a camera crew in your bedroom.
- You will hurt yourself.

THE COST OF FREE SPEECH

Most of us grew up in a country where you have a lot of freedom. Yes, of course, there are laws to prevent you from doing stupid things like running down Main Street in your birthday suit yelling, "Who wants to blow out the candle?" But within reason you can pretty much say whatever you want without fear of imprisonment.

However, as a married man you will soon learn that there are things worse than imprisonment. For example, sharing a home with a woman who finds you annoying. So over time you will figure out that you need to really think about not only what you're going to say but how you're going to say it.

Let me help you speed up that process. There is no acceptable way to mention certain things. For example, your wife's weight gain. You certainly can't be blunt, and you might think it's cute to encapsulate the thought inside a witty comment like "You're a lot stronger than you used to be. I never thought you'd be able to lift over 200 pounds, and now you do it every time you stand up." But it's not. You can say it about someone else and she'll laugh like crazy. You just can't say it about her. In fact, you can't say anything negative about her.

She already knows she's gained weight. She gets constant reminders from her clothes and full-length mirrors and those tiny airplane seats. You're her last hope. She thinks you either haven't noticed or don't mind if she gets fat. When you take that away, you're looking for trouble.

Now, I know what you're going to say: your wife should be a responsible, confident adult and have the inner strength to keep herself fit and happy and looking good. Do you honestly think a woman who was that balanced and capable would be attracted to you? Of course not.

Your wife has weaknesses, just like the rest of us. Which includes you. So you have to take the high road here. You have to see yourself as a support system for your wife. Try to say things that focus on the positive. But don't overdo it. And don't include any of her physical attributes in your compliments, particularly if you like to use the word *huge*. And don't go too far the other way, either, by giving her a compliment that's so lame it's almost an insult. Like, "You can do a lot of stuff with your left hand." Or "I really like your right knee. It's huge."

Sometimes you'll see couples who've been married a long time and you'll notice that the husband hardly ever talks. It's not bad manners, it's self-preservation. He's decided, based on experience, that he's better off being criticized for not talking than being ostracized for what he says. The best advice I can give you is to make sure your actions and words are completely in sync with how you truly feel.

If you like your wife and want to stay with her, don't give her a cheap shot, no matter how much it entertains your unhappily married friends. Nobody's perfect, but if you can stay consistent, that may be close enough.

THE GREATER GOOD

As the veterinarian said to the pregnant moose, I don't want this to come out the wrong way. However, there are times when telling the truth, or at least the whole truth so help you God, is not in anyone's best interest. For example, when you're coming home unexpectedly late—unexpectedly *really* late—and you didn't call. You meant to call. You even thought of it, but the time was never right—one of your buddies had just started into a really long joke or the food was coming and you didn't want the waitress at Hooters to know you're married. Whatever the excuse, you know you were wrong not to call. And you also know that at this particular moment, the truth is not your friend.

In fact, when you think about it, the truth is not even correct. Because the truth is she regards your not calling as a sign that you don't care about her and that your relationship is not important to you. You know that's not correct. You *do* care about her and your relationship *is* important, and you don't want her to be angry with you, especially if you fall asleep before she does.

So what you want to send is a message that reflects how you truly feel. The truth doesn't do that. The truth reflects a stupid mistake you made, and if it is revealed, nobody wins. She ends up hurt and feeling unimportant. You end up in big trouble. So this is one of those times in life when you have to focus on the greater good. It's better for both of you if she sees your lack of communication as an unavoidable incident brought on by extraordinary circumstances, rather than the thoughtless actions of a stupid, stupid man. It's better for both of you if you lie.

Step one: reset the clock on your cellphone to four in the afternoon. Then toss it forward out the car window and run over it. Stop and pick it up. With any luck the clock will still display the time of death.

Now drive to a very busy street within walking distance of your house, abandon the car and walk towards your home—but don't go home. Stop at a buddy's house. If his wife is home, go to the next house. As soon as you find one with a man alone in it, ask if you can use the phone.

Call your wife and tell her a story involving car accidents and traffic jams, all the while ignoring your buddy smirking and giving you the thumbs up. Keep the story short and don't give a lot of details. Your verbiage and credibility are inversely proportional. And stay in the realm of the plausible. When she asks you what caused the accident, say you don't know. Don't start speculating about a jaywalking Sasquatch. When she asks why you didn't call earlier, start crying and tell her about your cellphone and the UPS truck that ran over it.

If she buys the story and says she's been worried sick, apologize.

Don't say it wasn't your fault before she does. If she says she kept dinner warm, thank her and admit that you're starving, even though you've just eaten your weight in chicken wings. Then rush home, hug her and kiss her, chow down whatever she's made and tell her how this whole chain of events has reminded you of how much you care about her. Always good to at least end with the truth.

THE HOW AND THE WHY

For just this brief moment, I am going to draw from my own personal experience. This is something that happened to me in my own marriage. If my wife or any of her friends are reading this book, which is incredibly unlikely, rest assured that absolutely nothing else in this book bears any resemblance to anything that has ever occurred between my wife and myself in the past or at any time in the future.

So here's the thing I noticed: whenever my wife would ask me a simple question like "Have you seen the car keys?" or "What's the name of the neighbours' dog?" or "Did you buy a lottery ticket?" I would give straightforward, specific, direct answers like "They're on the hook by the back door." Or "Sparky." Or "Yes." However, my wife never does that. No matter what I ask or when I ask or how many times I ask, I always get the same answer: "Why?"

I find that very odd. For example: "Where's the can of lawn mower gas?" Answer: "Why?" What do you mean, "Why?" Are you going to change or withhold your answer, based on what I want to know for? The word *why* is pretty small, but the implications are huge. When somebody asks you why, it can mean a lot. For example, it can mean:

- You can't be trusted.
- It's not good for you to know that.

- I'll decide what you should and shouldn't do.
- I'm going to try my best to prevent a disaster.
- I've seen you do stupid things before.
- The world relies on me to control you.
- I will not visit you in prison.

But actually, the word *why* is revealing of yet another challenge in the complex nature of male–female interaction. Men are naturally curious about how things work. When they see a lift bridge, they'll watch it operate nine or ten times, ignoring the honking cars as they stare at different parts of it through each cycle until they figure out how each component plays a role in the overall task of raising and lowering the bridge. A woman, on the other hand, will be staring at her watch, wondering how much longer until she can drive over this stupid thing. She doesn't care how it works. She understands *why* it works: so boats can go by, now get on with it. Men don't care why it works, they just think it's neat and want to know *how* it works in case they ever want to do something neat in their lives, should their wives let them.

Men are theoretical; women are practical. And women are fine with that. You can theorize and pontificate until you're blue in the face. The trouble starts when you put those theories into action. Like building a lock-and-dam system between the above-ground pool and the fish pond. Someone needs to prevent that from happening. Someone needs to nip it in the bud. When you ask, "Have you seen the cable and pulleys from the old clothesline?" someone needs to ask, "Why?" And someone does.

THE SECRET PANEL

One of the most daunting challenges a new husband faces is to be able to detect when something is wrong in the relationship.

And once detected, he must then be able to deduce the events that led to the rift, and from there, come up with a strategy that brings the two of them back together. I brought a panel of married guys together and set up hypothetical situations to see how they do when facing these types of problems. Here are the results:

Scenario One

A husband and wife are out for dinner with friends. He asks her to tell the story about when she did some incredibly dumb thing at the supermarket and came home smelling like dill pickles. She says she'll tell it later, but right now wants to hear everybody else's news. He reminds her four more times through dinner, but she keeps postponing it. Finally, when the bill arrives, he can't hold it any longer and tells the story himself, complete with lots of theatrics— he uses his full repertoire of exaggerated facial expressions and even gets out of his chair to do the splits with a foot on each pickle. It's a stellar performance and everybody is in hysterics, with the exception of his wife. There is a cold silence all the way home in the car, and when his wife gets into bed, the furnace kicks on. What is wrong with his wife, how did it happen and what should he do now to make it right?

MOOSE T.: I have no idea.

STINKY P.: It sounds to me like this guy's wife has no sense of humour. My wife's like that too. Not sure how you fix that. I usually try telling more jokes until I get one she likes. Never have.

BUSTER H.: She didn't want to tell the story. Almost everyone has a fear of public speaking. Then, when he took the heat on her behalf by showing how effective public speaking can be when you tell a good story with poise and confidence, she was upset because it was her story but he got all the glory. The only

way he can make it right now is the next time
they're in a similar situation, he needs to get
everybody at the table to insist she tell the story.
That's what I'd do.

JUNIOR S.: I think you guys have all missed the point here.
She didn't want anybody telling that story. It's
an embarrassing story and it makes her look like
an idiot. And it's even worse that her husband
told it, because he's supposed to be the guy who
loves her the most and he's the one making her
look stupid. He needs to apologize and then he
needs to do something way stupider than she's
ever done and then let her tell the story to
everybody. It's okay if your wife is stupid as
long as you're stupider.

Scenario Two

The guys asked him to join them for a beer after work. They'd
never asked him before, so he was flattered. So there he is, having
a good time plowing through nachos and draft beer, when his cellphone rings. He doesn't answer it because that would be rude, but
he sees it's his wife calling and he suddenly remembers he was supposed to pick her up at the hairdresser's so the two of them could
shop for a new living room set. He downs his beer and takes off.
He drives like a madman, but he's still two hours late and his wife
is ticked. She wants to know what happened and why he didn't
even answer when she called. He lies. He tells her the car broke
down and the road was closed and the battery went dead on his
cellphone. Suddenly, his wife's cellphone rings. She answers. It's
the waitress from Hooters dialing the last number received on the
cellphone he left there. His wife gives him a look that would curdle
cheese and storms out of the house. What now?

MOOSE T.: We don't have a Hooters in our town.

JUNIOR S.: I think this guy needs to put his foot down. He finally gets asked to go out for a beer and she gets her nose all out of joint. He's gotta just stand up to her and say a man's gotta do what a man's gotta do. That's what he should do. Mind ya, I wouldn't try it.

BUSTER H.: I don't think she's upset about him forgetting to pick her up. It's the lying she's mad at. And I don't blame her. If you're gonna lie, you gotta do a lot better job than this guy did. She deserves a better lie than that one.

STINKY P.: This goof made his big mistake a long time ago. He's convinced his wife he's a guy who remembers things like appointments or birthdays or anniversaries. That's just an argument waiting to happen. You gotta let your wife know that you've got a mind like a sieve. You can't remember anything. The last thing you say before going to work is "Be sure to call me and remind me about picking you up after work. Love ya."

Scenario Three

They go to a street party to welcome a new neighbour. She's an attractive blonde divorcée. They both introduce themselves and then move along to greet other couples, but the husband doubles back to offer the new neighbour a drink. He chats with her a few times through the evening and even dances with her, although there is no music. Later, when he's walking home with his wife, she innocently asks him what he thinks of the new neighbour. He says he didn't really pay that much attention to her. Thus begins World War III. Where did he go wrong and how does he fix it?

MOOSE T.:	Do you have any pictures of the blonde?
STINKY P.:	This guy broke a cardinal rule. You should never meet attractive single women when your wife is there. You have to either meet them alone or not at all. The bankrupt ex-husbands I know would recommend not at all. And the biggest problem is that this guy's wife now thinks he's like that with every unattached woman he meets. The only way he can rebuild her trust is to quit his job and stay home for a year without ever opening the mail or talking on the phone.
JUNIOR S.:	This is a tough one, but I tell ya, apologizing is not the way to go. He's gonna think he's apologizing for his behavior, but he's actually apologizing for his intentions. But his intentions aren't going to change and it only hurts his case to draw attention to them. I recommend he goes with a full-court bluff. Tell her he's shocked that his wife would prefer him to shun this new neighbour rather than welcome her. The Bible says you should love thy neighbour. Flirting with her was just the Christian thing to do. That's what I'd try—it worked for Jimmy Swaggart.
BUSTER H.:	This is one of these unfortunate situations when lying won't work. Instead, I recommend this guy tells his wife he has a friend that's looking to hook up with a woman and he was just scouting this new neighbour out on that friend's behalf. That may be a lie right now, but as soon as he finds a friend in that situation, it won't be. Any statement that becomes true eventually is not a lie.

THE ANSWER IS BLOWIN' IN THE WIND

If any man truly wants to have a close and lasting relationship with a woman, he must make a concerted effort to change his behaviour and attitude. That's because men instinctively see things differently than women do, and women don't like that. Sometimes with men it's a maturity issue, a matter of putting aside childish things. In short, a man needs to stop saying and doing anything that his wife finds "inappropriate."

I could give many examples of these divisive behaviours, but there is nothing that better exemplifies the difference between men and women than their attitude towards flatulence.

And to be honest, I'm with the women on this one. There is nothing acceptable about flatulence. It is a social error. Yes, it's organic. I'm sure it happens to every animal with a digestive system. Just looking at a hippo, you can almost hear the flatulence. But a hippo doesn't raise one leg and almost give himself a hernia trying to make it really, really loud. Only men do that.

That's just wrong. Flatulence is to be stifled, not amplified. Or elongated. If it's unavoidable, okay, we can all accept that, but you need to immediately go somewhere private, like a restroom, and get it over with as quickly and quietly as possible. Nobody finds it amusing when you use it as a performance opportunity. Like when you wait until you're in a tunnel to get the best acoustics, or until everyone is quiet in church.

People don't want to hear anything your large intestine has to say. There should be a full stop at every colon.

For a mature, responsible person, like your wife, flatulence is a crude, undignified display of childishness and bad manners. For most men, it's a source of great pride and unrelenting humour. At its genesis, flatulence is an act of aggression—an assault on two of the senses. Even more if you do the laundry. Your wife does not want to be with a man who acts like a nine-year-old, or even worse, a nine-year-old Clydesdale. Women do not enjoy bathroom humour. Only a man would let out a loud blast of wind and then say, "I'd rather have an empty house than a bad tenant" or "Did somebody step on a duck?" No woman would do that. You can't imagine Queen Elizabeth saying that. But Prince Philip might. Although he'd give it the royal touch— "Did somebody step on a swan?"

As men, we all need to grow up and earn the love and respect of our wives and children. You've got to set a good example. Like father, like son. He'll do what you do, and he's younger and stronger, so it'll be louder and longer. Is that the legacy you want to leave to the world? (I know a part of you wants to say yes, but you must fight that.) Flatulence is a sign of disrespect and it's destroying the ozone. So the next time it happens, don't exploit it with wild gyrations and facial contortions and then explode in uncontrollable laughter. Just excuse yourself and light a match.

AND BABY MAKES THREE

In the first few years of marriage, you'll have a lot of good times. And chances are, nine months after one of those good times, you're going to find out that you and your wife are pregnant.

It will be a shock to you. This is something that you never realistically considered because of its potential negative impact on those aforementioned good times. There is no greater reminder of the fundamental tenet of cause and effect than finding out you are "with child." Well, maybe not you specifically, but someone very close to you—in fact, as close as you can get. Both of you are about to go through some life-altering experiences. Especially her. So hang on, you could be in for a bumpy ride.

Of course, both of you are going to have a positive first reaction to the news. For your wife, it taps into the natural mothering instincts that may have been what drew her to you. For you, you have that hardwired burst of pride that you are a stud.

You promised your wife that together the two of you would grow and prosper, and now your numbers are about to go up by 50 per cent. That's a great return on investment. They say that nothing worthwhile in life comes easy. In my experience, even things that are a complete waste of time can be difficult. But having a baby is an extra challenge.

The first issue is all the things that are going to happen to your wife's body and mind over the next nine months, and possibly twenty-one years. Yes, her skin will clear up and her hair will have lustre and her smile will glow, but she'll also put on fifty pounds, have a sore back and never be more than a hundred feet from the restroom. It's commonly known that pregnant women look beautiful, but not to them. If your wife has always prided herself on looking good and being fit, it may be hard for her to see herself resembling a gecko that swallowed a bowling ball.

And she will be tired all the time. It won't be just you napping anymore. The worst part is she may get depressed. And you not only have to accept all of these developments, you have to accept them *appreciatively*. This is not a time for you to be negative or even neutral. You must be constantly positive and supportive. You should overhear total strangers commenting to each other about what a perfect husband and soon-to-be father you are. You need to build and then maintain all of the goodwill you can muster. That's because, under all the pain and medical issues and bouts of depression, at the very core of her being, SHE BLAMES YOU. And she's right. So don't push your luck.

You've got to find a way to survive the next nine months. And she's probably given up drinking, which doesn't help. And you're probably drinking more, which *really* doesn't help. I suggest that, for the entire term of the pregnancy, you stop thinking of your-selves as a married couple, but rather as a company that has just been awarded a contract to build a new person and to deliver that person in brand-new condition, on time and on budget. And if you do it right, you get to keep it. And if you do it wrong, you get to keep it longer.

LABOUR DISPUTES

Everybody knows that delivering a baby is not easy, and sometimes, in the heat of battle, a woman will say hateful things to her husband that he must find a way to ignore. She doesn't mean any harm; it's just that she feels a couple should experience everything as equal partners, and at this particular moment he doesn't seem to be getting his fair share. Here are a few examples of things your wife may say to you at the moment of truth:

- "I've decided not to do this."
- "This can't be right."
- "When I'm reincarnated, I'm going to come back as a man and marry you and we're gonna have fourteen kids."
- "Change your clothes. I don't want the baby to meet you in that shirt."
- "When this is over I'm going to feed you cheese for a month and we'll see how _you_ like it."
- "This baby better look like me."
- "Don't you ever come near me again."
- "Don't look at me with those eyes."
- "Don't you dare smile."
- "We're not naming the baby after your mom."
- "If I get through this, I'm taking the rest of my life off."

A SMALL ADJUSTMENT

After the baby arrives and all is well, the three of you will go home together and start a radically different life. For starters, your days of sleeping with your wife are over. In fact, your days of sleeping *at all* are over. That's because you have just been appointed the personal valet to a small being who has no patience, constant needs and a very loud voice.

You'll be surprised by the strength and persistence of this new life force that has entered your world. You'll also be surprised at how fast the baby grows. And it does that by processing a lot of milk through a very small digestive system, which means there's a fair amount of exhaust. Actually, an unfair amount of exhaust.

Now, if you're a caring father, you will have informed your wife about all the benefits of breastfeeding, even though you will leave out the biggest benefit, which is that she's the one who has to do it. So to make up for that inequality, your wife may suggest, in a steely-eyed, don't-mess-with-me kind of way, that you should do the lion's share of the diaper duty. You may be a little squeamish at first, but you will eventually get your sea legs and may even get to the point where you can change the baby while eating a bowl of stew.

But the irony of all of this is that the baby is changing you a lot more than you're changing the baby. That's because everything in your marriage has shifted. There's a new focus, and it ain't you.

That can be a good thing. You can get away with stuff when you're not the centre of attention. Record those half-hour shows that your wife won't let you watch, like *Swamp Gas* or *Those Crazy Wankers*. Then, while your wife is doing the twenty-minute breastfeeding, you can fast-forward through the commercials and watch the whole show before it's time to change the baby again.

Other than those moments, you and your wife are in survival mode. This baby thing is a huge commitment. It will take most of your energy and most of your resources, both financial and emotional. You need to make sure that your wife knows you see this as a team effort. It's like any great invention—you can't just be there for the conception and then hand it over to the hired help. You've got to see it through.

Sure, you may eventually get to your wits' end, but your wife will be there with you, and sometimes it's easier for two people to find their way back together. On the really dark days, be sure to remind her how much the baby looks like her. In time, the good days will far outnumber the bad.

Throughout the history of the world there've been at least fifty couples who didn't resent having children. More couples resent *not* having them. So I'd say we're just a resentful species.

And the weird thing is that when your baby gets to be two or three years old and you're both being run off your feet, the best solution is to have another one. Sure, it'll be a couple of years of hell, but after that they'll be able to tire each other out and you and your wife can get back to being a married couple.

And think of the memories you get from having kids. Nobody sits around in rest homes reminiscing about the time they changed a head gasket on a big-block V8. They think about their kids. And wonder why they don't visit more often.

LETTER FROM BUSTER

Dear Red, Moose, Stinky, Flinty and any other potential friend that I might otherwise have met over the next three years or so,

I'm writing to inform each of you that I will unfortunately not be able to attend our annual Fishing Derby this weekend, or the one next year or the one after that or maybe ever again for the rest of my natural life. I'm saying this even though we all know I won the derby last year with that largemouth bass.

This is because my wife gave birth to our first child last night. I'm sure many of you heard the screaming. My wife has a pretty good set of lungs. So I'm out of the derby. I've got to focus on the baby. It was a little over twenty-seven pounds and measured fourteen inches in girth just below the gills. Man, that was some bass. Probably wouldn't catch anything that big this year anyway . . . But the truth is I'm a father now and I need to accept that.

I gotta say, it was not an easy delivery. First thing that went wrong, she comes to me and starts yelling that she's got to go to the hospital like right then. She wasn't interested in waiting until the end of overtime or even the next commercial. So I shut off the TV, and it wasn't easy setting the DVR with her screaming in my ear. Next she tells me that I'll need to put some pants on because she's expecting me to come into the hospital with her rather than just drop her off, which I had always understood to be the plan. I complained that there'd be nothing for me to do, but she said they had a TV in the waiting room. So off we go.

Well, she was on my case the whole drive over there. If it wasn't the speed bumps, it was the potholes—nothing seemed to please her. When we got to the hospital, the nurse asked me how dilated she was. I said I don't know for sure, but I've never seen her eyes that wide open so I'd take that as a clue. The next thing you know they're handing me a mask and hospital gown. I told them I can't do this. I don't even bait my own hooks. They said the doctor would be there. I was just going in to witness the birth. Hey, I would have taken their word for it. All they had to do was come out of the delivery room with a baby and I'd have a pretty good idea where it came from. But oh no, I had to be there.

After that, things moved pretty fast. The nurses relayed the doctor's instructions. When it was time, I pushed as hard as I could but the door opened in, so I was trapped. Somebody grabbed me and walked me around to where I could see the baby pop out, and I gotta tell you, it's going to take a long time for me to get that visual de-welded from my brain. The first thing out was the head. It looked like a watermelon coming through an O-ring. Now, I guess for the doctor, it's something he sees every day (another reason not to be a doctor), but for me it was pretty traumatic. You know how they say in battle some soldiers just get a rush of adrenaline and do something they wouldn't ordinarily be capable of? That's what I did. I've never passed out before. Didn't even stay conscious long enough to see if the baby was a pointer or a setter.

Anyway, I'm sure I'll be back to my normal self in a few days. Not sure I want to have another baby for a while. Maybe you guys could drop by after the derby. I sure wouldn't mind seeing a picture of the winning fish.

Your ex-fishing buddy,

Buster

DO AS I SAY

As your child learns to walk and talk and have real underwear, you will eventually become aware that this is another completely separate human being with their own agenda and the willpower to get it done.

I know the easy way out is to just let the kid do whatever it wants, but you'll end up having a miserable life and the child will never develop the characteristics required for success in school or in business or in life, and consequently that child will never move out.

You don't want that. So you need to do something *now* to prevent that from happening later. You're going to have to discipline the child. And I'm sorry to have to tell you this, but that's going to take a significant effort from you over a considerable period of time.

The sad truth is that the first step in disciplining a child requires that you begin by disciplining yourself. You have to decide what the rules are and then you have to have the guts to enforce them consistently forever. Sometimes it's just easier to open another six-pack and turn up the TV.

But let's assume that you've finally decided that letting your child run wild has lost its appeal. You're tired of the broken toys and crayons on the walls and the food on the ceiling. It's time for a little tough love.

Now, there are situations in your life where you need to be all by yourself, reviewing all the information and devising a plan that will allow you to reach the desired goal. This is not one of those. This is a time where you need your wife to help you build it. You can't work as a team if you don't *start* as a team.

First step: Do you both agree that it's in everyone's best interest for the child to have rules? Yes. Next: Are you willing to use discipline to make that happen? Sure . . . I guess so. Next: What specific form of discipline are you willing to enforce? This will take some discussion. Might be good to have the Penal Code handy. And finally: Are you prepared to make a lifelong commitment to the plan, reviewing the rules regularly, making changes when necessary but always through discussion with your spouse, and most important, maintaining a consistent level of fair discipline, so help me God, till death do us part, amen? Now write that up and both of you sign it. Make three copies. One for you. One for her. One for the safety deposit box.

I know this sounds like overkill, but you both need a constant reminder or you will backslide. Discipline is really hard on most parents. There are a lot of reasons for that. For one thing, you probably weren't that great a kid and you really weren't disciplined effectively and you turned out okay, so the hell with it.

Plus, you feel guilty disciplining your own child when you did much worse things and got away with them.

Also, you have to deal with your kid's reaction to the discipline. They may not like it. They may resent you sending them to their room or taking the wheels off their bike or hiding their cigarettes. And they're shrewd. They will immediately go to their mother to see if she's as evil as you are. And they'll start with "Daddy hates me," implying that if Mom supports Dad, she must hate the kid too.

Mom doesn't want the kid to think that, so she caves. Or it could just as easily be the dad. We all want our kids to like us because they can easily slip under the kitchen table and bite you. So discipline is a tricky one.

Some people say discipline is an expression of love, but I've seen those movies with the whips and leather outfits and I'm not so sure. I would say consistent, reasonable discipline that's in the child's best interest is the way to go. But your wife has to be on board. If she doesn't want the kid to be disciplined, it ain't gonna happen. She'll just find ways to help him misbehave and you'll have to live with it. But when it eventually breaks up your marriage, if the judge is a man, he'll make sure she gets the kid.

GO IN PEACE

There is a flaw in the design of cars. It's due to the ever-changing role of the person in the passenger seat.

If you go back to the origins of the automobile, which is of course the horse-drawn wagon or Conestoga or stagecoach or chuck wagon (or, if you suffer from motion sickness, the upchuck wagon), you will discover that "riding shotgun" literally meant riding shotgun. The passenger's job was to watch for robbers and hijackers, give them a speedy trial and announce the verdict loud and clear through at least one of the barrels of a three aught three. Over time, most of the robbers decided to pursue safer careers, so the role of the passenger evolved from hired killer to navigator.

That role survived the transition to automobiles, and even as late as the 1970s you'd hear Mom either giving course corrections to Dad or clearing her throat really loudly to indicate he was going the wrong way. But of course, the advent of the GPS ended all that. The driver suddenly had an irrefutable, objective impersonal device that would take him anywhere and never make a judgment or hold a grudge.

The downside is that the passenger now had no constructive role in the driving experience. And yet they were there. Sitting right up in the front seat where they would have full access to the knobs that work the heater and the radio. And worst of all, they had time to talk to you and you were trapped behind the wheel and couldn't get away. It ended a lot of marriages.

Whenever I see a car that's run head-on into a bridge abutment or over a cliff, if there's a couple in the front seat I always question that it was an accident. And this is not a sexist opinion. It's the same situation when the wife is driving. The husband is nothing but a nuisance sitting there in the passenger seat, whistling or cleaning his toenails. And if the passenger is a nervous traveller, it's even worse—squeezing all the padding out of the armrest or stomping his or her foot down through the floorboards to indicate that the driver should maybe ease off on the throttle a tad.

So if you want your marriage to last and your travel to be pleasant, I suggest you do a major renovation on the passenger area in your car. When you have a newborn baby in a car seat, the manufacturers tell you to make sure the seat faces the rear of the car, as that will give the baby the most protection in an accident. So that's the first step. Remove the passenger seat, rotate it 180 degrees and reinstall it facing the rear window.

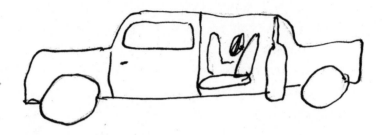

This simple move is a godsend for every driver. Instantly, the passenger is no longer aware of other traffic, so they can't give advice or criticism. Plus, they are facing away from all the dashboard controls that are rightfully your domain as the driver. It also makes conversation with the driver very difficult, but I've always found a talking driver is a dangerous driver. Particularly if they say something that may cause the passenger to throw a double cheeseburger at them and the dill pickle goes up one nostril.

Much safer to have your wife facing backwards, where she can talk face to face with the kids and you can just stay out of it. Also safer because she can keep an eye on the kids and throw the cheeseburger at *them* if necessary.

If you're lucky enough not to have kids, the whole back seat becomes her hobby centre/craft corner. Pick up a few of those miniature modular closets they sell in those Swedish stores that use the bearded guy in their ads, and you'll get so much storage space in the back seat, your wife will be making rural scene quilts and animal-shaped tea cozies well into the next millennium. She may suggest you install a vanity back there so she can do her hair and touch up her makeup and whatnot, but be very careful. A vanity always involves a mirror and that will allow her to see what you're up to, which defeats the whole purpose of the reconfiguration.

And if you're really handy, you can add pulleys and cables that will mechanize the whole setup so the cupboards all fold away into the trunk area when it's her turn to drive.

They'll be replaced with a modular flat-screen/DVD player that flips up on the window shelf, a cooler/hassock with vibrating foot massager in the lid and a 12-volt popcorn maker set at an angle that allows the popcorn to arc right into your mouth. (Unplug the machine if you're drowsy or if you have an enlarged nostril from the dill pickle incident.)

I realize every couple is different, and some can actually drive together in a normal front seat for upwards of fifteen minutes before having an altercation of some kind. But why take the chance? By investing a few dollars and a little time, you can make these simple changes and ensure that your marriage will last longer than the car payments.

SPARE THE ROD, SPARE THE DAD

So to recap—kids need a firm but gentle hand from both parents. There's always going to be a more lenient parent, though, and I recommend that you, as the father, should be the strict one. Children soon figure out which parent they have the best chance with, and if it's not you, your wife will be dealing with all the issues all the time while you'll be left alone on the couch to watch the game.

Your child may not like you as much as he or she likes Mom, but come the teenage years and the need for money, you'll get a lot more popular.

But be careful when you set the standard for how strict a parent you're going to be. Discipline should never be a hurtful thing. It should be used to guide the child into making decisions that will lead to a happier life. The only discomfort a child should feel is the temporary suspension of freedom as a reminder about cause and effect.

Yes, you understand that he/she was playing a video game and kept getting killed by cyborgs and that was getting frustrating, but throwing his/her favourite snack bowl at the flat-screen TV was not appropriate, and as a result he/she will be having a time-out until early next year.

But the biggest danger in you being a strong disciplinarian is that it sets a precedent for everyone in the family, including you. You're saying that if the child does something that's thoughtless or dangerous or hurtful, he/she needs to be punished so as to learn not to do those things anymore. Your wife will accept that. She'll even like it. She'll even like it so much that she will put you under the same scrutiny. And she has ways of punishing you that are much more effective than anything you can do to your child.

So once in a while you need to show some leniency. Let the kid off the hook. Call it a brain cramp, laugh it off, give a pat on the head and say, "Don't do it again."

But make sure your wife sees you do it, because you may be looking for that same treatment at some point in the future and it will be good to have a precedent.

TROUBLE AT SCHOOL

Because your son is not adopted or being raised by other parents, it's only a matter of time until you're going to get called into a meeting with his teacher. Your first reaction will be anger and disappointment with your son. Your wife will be embarrassed and guilty that the two of you have failed as parents.

It's your job to ignore those natural responses and instead come up with a plan that will convince the teacher it's *his* fault. That starts with the shock in your voice when the school calls you to set up the meeting. (See the section on faking surprise, elsewhere in this book.)

Prior to the meeting, you need to devise a plan that will lead the school to believe your son has great potential and that they are somehow dropping the ball. You and your wife need to work on this together.

You also need to look your best when going to the interview. Ask your wife to buy herself a nice new conservative outfit and to get her hair done. If you have hair, get it done too. It will probably go better if only one of you speaks during the interview, so decide which one that will be. Your wife is more liable to tell the truth, so I suggest *you* do the talking.

Ask your wife to give you examples of whenever your son has done something smart or kind. She may need a few days' warning. While you're waiting, you can call the parents of one of the good students and ask them where the school is. When it's time for the meeting, get to the school a half hour early so you can park far enough away that they can't see your vehicle.

Take a hip flask of bourbon so you can have a couple of bracers before going in. You and your wife need to walk into the school with your heads held high, implying the subtle message that something is not right with this establishment and you're going to get to the bottom of it.

Step up to the secretary's desk and tell her which teacher you're there to see. Hopefully, his name is still written on your hand from when you took the phone message. Use his name with respect throughout the interview. If it's Gibson, call him Mr. Gibson. Resist the temptation to start calling him Ace or Huckleberry.

Once the introductions are done and you all sit down for the meeting, you need to verify that Mr. Gibson has the right kid. Mention your son's name and show him a picture. If you don't have a picture, ask the teacher if *he* has one and identify your son from that. Or you could describe your son and see if that matches the kid Mr. Gibson is referring to. If you haven't seen your son for a month or more, keep the description more general and add an inch of height.

Once your son is identified, let the teacher know what a great kid what's-his-name is and that you and your wife are both baffled by the suggestion of problems at school. Every time Mr. Gibson hints your son may not have the ability or parental structure necessary to succeed in any subject, stonewall him. Tell him that your son comes from a long line of scholars. His great-great-great-grandfather had Galileo as a teacher and Archimedes as a principal.

If the teacher claims your son never interacts with people, point out that if that's true, how come every cop in town knows him by name? No matter what Mr. Gibson asks or tells, you stay on course—your son is a good boy and he's doing great everywhere except school. And then ask the teacher why that is. Put *him* on the defensive for a change.

When the interview is over and you're on your way home, your wife will say nice things to you. Oh sure, she'll be aware that you came across like a total idiot, but you'll be a total idiot who defends his wife and his son, and she likes that. Plus, it helps Mr. Gibson understand why the boy is the way he is. Yet another win-win.

THE FIRST FIGHT

Dear Diary,

Not a good day today. Buster Jr. (my wife calls him Douglas 'cause that's what she named him) got into a fight at school. I was okay with it at first, but then I found out he lost the fight. In my book, that's called "bullying." I didn't know the family but got their address out of the school directory and went to see them. The parents knew that Buster had started the fight so that was a setback. They called for the kid to come out and speak to me. She was a big girl and she looked like she could take care of herself. She looked like she could also take care of a large pizza. I suggested that maybe in the future she should pick on someone her own size, and I may have added "if there is such a person." All I know is she got upset. The father laughed, but the mother took a swing at me, so I got out of there. Like I say, not a good day, but Buster learned it's wrong to hit a woman.

YOU DA MAN

The day arrives for every father of a boy when his wife says to him, "You need to have a talk with your son." And not just any talk; *the* talk. The one about the birds and the bees, which has never been about actual birds and bees.

Your initial response will be negative. You don't feel comfortable talking to your thirteen-year-old son about sex. You talk to your guy friends about sex 24/7. Ninety-nine per cent of your joke repertoire is based on sex, and the other one isn't funny. You even make sexual innuendo–based comments to women, sometimes using the word *innuendo*. So it's not that you're uncomfortable talking about sex. You just don't want to talk to your son about it.

You also don't want to talk to your dad about it, which makes you feel that your son probably shares your reluctance. You hold the male default position that the important lessons in life are learned through experience rather than education. Let the kid just fumble along on his own like you did. If he doesn't know anything about sex, maybe he'll avoid it longer.

You have a million ways to justify your "don't ask, don't tell" approach. Unfortunately, they are all overruled by what your wife wants. And when your wife doesn't get what she wants, neither do you. If you won't talk about sex with your son, she won't talk about sex with you.

So I suggest you look for the good news in her request. First of all, it's a compliment to you that she thinks you have worthwhile knowledge and expertise in that area. Secondly, it prevents her from talking about the subject with your son, which might inadvertently reveal some inadequacies that will negatively impact your resumé. Lastly, think of how much more uncomfortable you would be talking about the subject with your teenage daughter, and you'll get a sense of why your wife needs you to do it.

So in the interest of family harmony and manning up, you need to have that talk. Yes, you're uncomfortable and you hate this, but it needs to be done, so here are a few tips to help avoid disaster:

- Don't try to dodge the bullet. Don't just hand him a medical book on the human body or a VHS cassette of a military training film on venereal diseases.
- Don't use metaphors or euphemisms. Don't talk about

trains going into tunnels or waves pounding the shore or the inner workings of a hydraulic pump.

- Use the animal kingdom as a reference. Take him to a cattle ranch in the spring. See if he has any questions. See if you have any answers.
- Be honest. Don't make jokes. That dog is not towing the other dog.
- Let him think that having children is the purpose of sex rather than an unfortunate side effect.
- Don't let him know how much fun it is. That thing is a tool, not a toy. Don't say that, either.
- Stay objective. Don't refer to things his mother likes.
- Keep it clinical. If you find yourself getting comfortable and starting to enjoy the subject, stop immediately.
- Don't scare him. The idea that his parents do this is frightening enough.
- Don't embarrass yourself unnecessarily. Let him start by asking questions. It's better for you to find out what he knows before he finds out what you don't know.
- Let him know that it's all perfectly natural and when he finds the right girl, it'll go great. Don't add that if he finds the wrong girl, it'll go even better. Let him know you're there for him, but there are limits on how far you'll go. Wish him well, give him a condom, but don't show him how to put it on. I'm sure he already knows.
- When your wife asks you how the sex talk went, tell her you need to do more research, then head for the bedroom.

LEVELS OF SURVEILLANCE

Any of you who have worked for, or been under the scrutiny of, the CIA, the FBI, the tax department or the hall monitor know that there are several levels of surveillance available for different applications. The higher the expected level of criminal activity, the higher the level of scrutiny.

This can mean more personnel covering a wider area for a longer period, more sophisticated equipment capable of intercepting more accurate information, and a multimedia approach capable of capturing all video, audio and even aromatic components. Naturally, these escalated levels of scrutiny require a much higher financial and political commitment from the management.

You need to know that your wife is capable of all of these levels of surveillance using nothing more than her own instincts and a few calls to some female friends. You may not believe me, because you've been fooled. You've been fooled by her into thinking that she really has no idea of or interest in, almost everything you say and do. I'm sorry to tell you that's just not true.

You got that impression because when you say things to her, she doesn't seem to pay much attention. Well, she's not interested in most of the things you say to her because she knows you're filtering and editing the information so that she won't be able to find fault. Perhaps you've noticed that your wife always hears everything you mumble under your breath. I've heard of cases where the only time a wife listens to her husband is when he's talking to himself. That's because women aren't nearly as interested in what they hear as they are in what they *over*hear.

Similarly, if any of us are involved in an accident or altercation of some kind, our wives are supportive but anxious to hear the story from an objective third party—particularly if that third party is a woman. That's because our wives think we lie. They think that because we do.

And they understand it. They understand that we don't want to look stupid or incompetent and that we hate to lose. We spend so much of our mental energy creating stories to make the dumb things we do look smart that we have no mental energy left to stop ourselves from doing more dumb things. It's the same reason wives pay very little attention to our normal day-to-day activities: so they can be ready to go into high alert when the time comes.

Our wives get caught between wanting to support our fragile egos and wanting to give us a shake for leaving them to pick up the pieces. That's why they amp up their level of scrutiny when they sense something unacceptable has just been said or done. It's because they'll be stuck with the consequences. Wives aren't trying to be critical; they're in damage-control mode.

Now, I guess there's a way to break this cycle, but it involves a man and a woman being more like each other, and where's the fun in that? Instead, I suggest we just leave things the way they are. You always feel better when you know why a car won't start, even if you can't fix it.

WHY IT TAKES HER SO LONG TO GET READY

For centuries, men have been puzzled over why it takes their wives so long to get ready to go out for an evening. And the fancier the occasion, the longer it takes. Men often fantasize about how many car engines they could have rebuilt or homes they could have renovated in the time spent waiting for their wives to be ready to go out. Sometimes husbands get snarky. Especially if it's an event they didn't particularly want to go to in the first place. They've gone out and started the car twice, and now it's getting ridiculous and they start honking the horn and yelling at the house. That's because they think their wife is taking so long because she's incapable of making a decision about what to wear, or she didn't think ahead, or she has unrealistic expectations about how good she can look, given enough time.

Only a really stupid husband mentions any of these theories, especially the last one. And sure, she may take longer deciding what dress to wear, which delays other decisions because the earrings and purse and shoes have to match, but that's not the real reason wives take longer to get ready.

Let me try to explain it in terms you'll understand. You know when you go to that deluxe car wash place in town? Where they have a full range of car wash options? If you're in a hurry—or cheap—you can just have the exterior wash where you drive away in a car that's somewhat clean and still wet. At the next level, they'll add hot wax and towel dry the car. Cleaning the wheels is another upgrade. Once in a while you might even splurge and get the inside of the car cleaned and vacuumed. After that, you get into the stratosphere of car cleaning. They don't even call it cleaning at that level, they call it "detailing." It's expensive, and you have to leave the car with them. Maybe for a full day, maybe longer. If it's been a while, they may have to remove the seats and pull out all the carpeting. Hey, don't look at me—*you're* the guy who drove down a gravel road drinking a quart of egg nog.

But here's my point: when *you* get ready to go out, you're having an exterior wash only, whereas your wife is being detailed. You're not curling your hair and putting on a foundation and lip gloss and eyeliner and mascara and blush and fingernail polish and toenail polish and shaving your legs. You went with the exterior wash—you're somewhat clean and still wet. She's on the deluxe plan and it takes time.

Stop complaining—you're not the victim here. The better she looks, the better you look. When she comes walking into the room behind you, she's the showboat, you're just the tug. So shut off the car, come back into the house and be damned glad that she still tries to look good. It's not pretty when you both give up.

THINGS TO THINK ABOUT WHILE WAITING FOR YOUR WIFE

- When they get married, the woman is thinking that from now on they can go on dates all the time. The man is thinking the exact opposite.
- It's difficult for me to anticipate what women are going to do or say because I find they think differently. And more often.
- As she gets older, your wife may start losing her short-term memory. This will ultimately save your marriage.
- Women have higher pain thresholds. A man could never survive childbirth or a bikini wax.
- Wives expect husbands to be good at sex, but they're not allowed to practice.
- We're supposed to be able to find the G-spot. We can't even find the jar of pickles in the fridge. And we put it in there.
- Your first exposure to a naked woman is like opening the hood of a hybrid. You don't see anything there that you recognize.
- If your wife is going through menopause, don't buy her a bathing suit and use her to heat the pool.

WOMANSPEAK

The English language is complex. The same words have different meanings in different contexts. And it's further complicated by coded messages that are used by women when talking to men. When women talk to each other, they are clear and obvious. When they talk to the main man in their lives, they are subtle and even obtuse. That's because they don't feel they should be saying what they're saying—rather, you should have figured out the issue and dealt with it all by yourself. We all know that's not going to happen, so the next best thing is for you to be able to interpret their messages.

When she says, "Do you know what the date is today?" she means, "You forgot our anniversary." When she says, "I saw your new receptionist," she means, "Fire her." When she says, "You go watch TV with your feet up while I make dinner," she means, "I dented the car." On the other hand, when she says, "I'll be ready in five minutes" or "You do whatever you want" or "I didn't buy anything," she's lying.

You may find that some of her statements challenge your decoding skills, but her questions are the real booby traps because they require a response from you. "What do you think I should do?" or "How does this outfit look?" or "What were you thinking?" This last question is getting dangerously close to being rhetorical. Rhetorical questions are the toughest because they mean that you're in big trouble and you don't know why and she's not going to help you find out. And most important, she does not want you to answer. Stop yourself from responding no matter how much you want to. When she says, "Are you trying to be funny?" I know you want to say yes, but it's not worth it. Believe me.

At the other end of the spectrum we find questions that need immediate and nonconfrontational answer. When she asks, "Do you think I'm an idiot?" don't wait a few seconds to think it over. Just say no. Or, even better, add, "We can't *both* be idiots." But be ready for an "Are you trying to be funny?"

My suggestion on dealing with this communication gap is to just give up. There's no chance you'll ever be able to understand what your wife means when she says anything. No means maybe, maybe means "I doubt it," and yes means "probably not." You'll never get it. So instead, go behind the words to the intentions. If she likes you, you don't need to understand her words. You're not in danger. So be kind and considerate and helpful and surprise her in good ways, and then get ready for the warm comments she sends your way, even though you won't have a clue what she's saying.

THE SHOPPER STOPPER

Chances are at some point you're going to face some financial challenges in your relationship. The small blips may involve a few bucks from Mom and Dad or even a cash advance from one of those payday loan places. But despite your best efforts, you may find that you're having a hard time staying afloat. You've maxed out your credit cards and you're making the minimum payments wherever possible, but at the end of the month there always seems to be a bill or two that has to wait. And if you get hit with a surprise—say, the car blew up or you forgot that this country has income tax—you really get behind the 8-ball.

The problem, of course, is very simple: you're spending more than you make. It's the solution that's tricky.

Some people try to go on a budget. They start with their monthly income and then they deduct their regular monthly expenses, and if there's anything left over, they can blow that. I know that's mature and logical, but it's not fun. In fact, it's annoying.

If, for example, you and your wife have a joint monthly income of $5,000, but once you deduct your taxes and your rent and your utilities and your groceries and your car payment and your credit cards, you find yourselves left with seventy-nine cents, you're not going to be happy. When you're not happy, bad things happen. And when your *wife's* not happy, *horrible* things happen.

Now, I know financial advisers will tell you to make an adjustment. Increase your income or switch to a cheaper home and car. This is why financial advisers have unhappy marriages. You don't want to do any of that stuff. Sure, you'd be solvent, but you'd be living in a dump and driving a Yugo.

So before you start taking drastic steps, here's a little something you can try. I'm going to suggest that one of you is a shopaholic—someone who buys things not because they need or even want them, but because it's just fun to buy things. Let's say that person is your wife, for argument's sake. (And who doesn't enjoy a good argument?) You can talk to her about financial shortfalls and budgets and debtor's prison until you're blue in the face, but she's going to find a way to buy things as long as she can get away with it. So not letting her get away with it becomes your primary objective.

And make no mistake: over the years she's gotten really good at hiding her purchases. Her own mother taught her well and she's taken the game up a notch or two. Have you noticed that when she comes home, she doesn't say where she's been? And if you ask her, she'll come up with a legitimate errand—going to the doctor or visiting a friend or whatever—but she will leave out one major detail: SHE ALSO STOPPED IN AT THE MALL.

You may be concerned when she comes into the house with a shopping bag because it means she bought something. Don't worry about it. It's when she comes in with *no* shopping bag that you're really in trouble. That means she's hidden everything in the trunk or under the hood, waiting until you go out before sneaking them into the house. And once the things are in there, she'll wait six months or more before wearing any of them, so when you ask her if that's a new dress, she'll say no, she's had it forever.

She may even bring her friend's purchases in, saying she's holding them so the friend's husband doesn't know. You need to realize that her friend is probably doing the same thing for her.

Now, I know you're thinking, "Okay, I realize my wife is a shopaholic but what do I do about it?" Well, you'll have to be a man here, which means that, rather than confront her and start a fight that will soon escalate into nuclear proportions, you need to contact her credit card company and lower the spending limit to something you can handle. When her card is refused, she'll be annoyed and embarrassed, but she can't even mention it to you because she's not supposed to be buying anything. And she still gets to spend something and it's manageable.

It's like owning an old boat. As long as the bilge pump is stronger than the leak, you're fine.

FINAL ANSWER?

They've always said it's a woman's prerogative to change her mind. It's not only true, it's also how most men got to learn what the word *prerogative* means. It's also why husbands spend so much of their lives rearranging furniture.

On the surface, it may seem like a pretty simple thing to fix. You probably think the reason women change their minds so often is because they don't put enough time and effort into the original decision. The inference is that only bad decisions need to be changed and that if you do your homework and take the process seriously, the decisions will be permanent.

This is a great theory, and like many great theories, it's incorrect. Women changing their minds is not based on making wrong decisions any more than men *not* changing their minds is based on making *right* ones. The reason men don't change their minds is because they can't be bothered. They thought about the situation, they looked at all the parameters, they made a decision, it's done, they've moved on. They will continue to carry out that decision until the evidence is overwhelming that it's just plain not working. It has more to do with laziness than with consistency, determination, reliability or persistence.

Similarly, a woman's reluctance to commit to a decision has more to do with her decision-making process than it has to do with flightiness or irresponsibility. It may be as basic as ego. A man has more than enough self-confidence to be able to make a decision and then see it through. He is not filled with self-doubt and feels no pressure to revisit the decision once it's been made. He sees the world as a relatively static place, where conditions remain the same while he's moving forward. A woman, on the other hand, sees the world as kinetic—everything is moving.

The earth spins on its axis while orbiting the sun, every body she knows is in motion, except maybe yours. Even her emotions and physical state are constantly changing. And almost all of these factors affect her decisions.

To her, if conditions change every day, if not every hour, how can you assume a decision that was made yesterday or last week or last month will still be the best answer? A woman says you can't. You need to be constantly monitoring all the changing parameters and continually re-evaluating your decisions based on the most current information. It's not irresponsibility, it's a relentless scientific quest to do the right thing using up-to-the-minute data.

I'm not saying it's right or it's wrong, because I'm married and I know better. I'm just saying it's a different process. Don't even ask your wife for a decision for anything that's going to happen in the future. Whether it's a holiday next month or a new car in the fall, no matter what she says, make sure your deposit is refundable. Things could change.

In fact, don't even phrase it as a decision; just ask her what she's thinking now. And keep asking that until the day of the event, which is when her answer will become a decision. And don't make a big deal out of it. Remember, she is constantly reviewing all of her decisions, even the one that brought the two of you together.

HOV

They repainted the stripes on our local highway. And when they did, they created a special lane between the fast lane and the median. They called it the HOV lane. I know it meant only certain cars could use it, so I tried to guess what HOV stood for—Herb's Old Volvo, Hispanics on Vacation, Husbands on Viagra. Eventually, my wife informed me in a fairly loud voice that it stood for High-Occupancy Vehicles, and if you had two or more people in your car you got to use this new express lane.

Well, okay, I guess that makes sense, but if you think about it for a few minutes, there's some flawed reasoning going on here. I understand the environmental impact of carpooling, but I don't think people drive as well when they have a passenger. They don't focus as much when they have someone to talk to. And why did they set aside the *passing* lane for HOVs? You think the fastest guy on the road will be the one who's talking to his friend about his favourite *Jerry Springer* episode?

And what happens when this guy suddenly realizes he needs to get off at the next exit? He cuts across all the other lanes, many of which are—or *were*—going faster than he is. And I think I was wrong to say "his friend" because most of the time it's not his friend sitting beside him, it's his wife. That's another flaw in the plan. Not one man I know drives faster with his wife in the car.

And they've got big double lines to stop you from switching lanes. They limit your access to get into the HOV lane, which also limits your ability to get out of the HOV lane—like, say, when a guy and his friend are tailgating you and your wife.

The HOV lane is to get people to travel together by rewarding them with their own path. It's not working because it's not enough of a reward. But mainly because it's too subtle. Men aren't good with subtle. Just tell us what you want, or even better, what to do, and we'll take it from there. Don't ask us to guess because chances are we'll guess wrong. They don't really care if we travel together; what they really want is to reduce the number of cars on the road.

So I say we do that by reducing the number of cars on the road. If the experts can tell us how many people can safely ride on an elevator, they can probably tell us how many cars can safely ride on a highway. Let's say it's ten thousand. They should just install an automatic gate at every highway entrance, as well as a counter. Also put a counter at every exit. Then you hook 'em all up to a central computer. As soon as the counters add up to ten thousand, all the gates close until somebody gets off the highway. Eventually, people will start travelling in non-peak times and will even carpool.

Especially men. We're not good at seeking reward, but we have a lot of experience avoiding punishment.

YOU AND THEM

They have these TV shows where all the players are divided into teams and given tasks, and at the end of every episode somebody gets fired or kicked off the island or announces that they're gay. The premise is based on making friends initially and then, over time, finding enough things wrong with the other person that you never want to see them again.

When you put most people in a situation where it comes down to survival, they will promote themselves and throw the other person under the bus. They will usually choose murder over suicide. These shows do a lot of damage by reminding us of that. It's a weekly message that it's a dog-eat-dog world out there and you need to be constantly scheming and manipulating to make sure you come out on top.

That's not good. Especially if you try to apply those principles to your family life.

Let's say, for example, that you are married with two kids. You'd like to purchase something fun. Specifically, an all-terrain amphibious vehicle that happens to be for sale at that store that sells stuff for men who are either single or recently divorced.

Sadly, your wife does not share your enthusiasm for applying the family's limited resources to this particular acquisition.

In a normal world, you would just let it go and rationalize how you can live without this toy. You might even try to get one of your single or recently divorced friends to buy it. But because of the influence of these TV shows, you may be tempted to form some kind of alliance with your children for the purpose of over-throwing your wife as chief financial officer of the nest egg.

If you have two sons, it will be easy. You can sneak them into the garage and show them pictures and demonstration videos. Maybe take them for a drive and casually drop by the dealership, where they can sit in the thing. You can even tell them you don't need a licence to operate amphibious vehicles, implying they could take turns driving this baby long before their sixteenth birthday. You could make up stories about all the adventures you could have.

Just make sure that the central and vital component in all of these adventures is the vehicle itself. It won't be a problem con-vincing them, because they're boys—and, even better, they're *your* boys. If you have a daughter, it's trickier. For some inexpli-cable reason, she, like her mother, will have no natural interest in this thing you feel you can't live without. So you have to lie to her. Don't feel bad; she does it to you all the time. From her brother, find out the name of the most popular boy at school. Tell your daughter that this boy was looking at the same amphibious vehicle you were, but his parents couldn't afford it. Tell her that you told the boy that if you bought it, he'd be welcome to join you any time you went out in it. My guess is your daughter will now be onside. But you have to move quickly before she gets a chance to talk to that boy.

So now the three of you are ready to present the proposal to Mom. Do it at the dinner table. Let your son take the lead, with his sister in support and you lagging behind like an objective observer. For your wife to say no, she'll have to disappoint all three of you.

Now, I know it looks fine when they do it on TV, but in real life there are a few problems with this approach to family decisions. First of all, it won't work. Just because your wife married you doesn't mean she's stupid. Second, it will divide the family in a way that puts you on a different side than your wife. That's never in your best interest. Even if you succeed in getting the vehicle, the kids will turn against you. Just like on the TV shows, you'll find out that their vision of using the toy didn't include you. The boy wants to drive it around on his own and the girl wants to be off in the woods with Lover Boy, not her dad. You'll be voted off the ATV.

And most important, years from now your wife will be sitting quietly and thinking about how lucky she is and what a great guy you are, when she'll suddenly remember that time you tried to use the kids to pressure her into doing something dumb. So be a man and learn to live without the toy. They may call it amphibious, but once you buy it, you're sunk.

FIVE REASONS YOUR WIFE IS NOT TALKING TO YOU

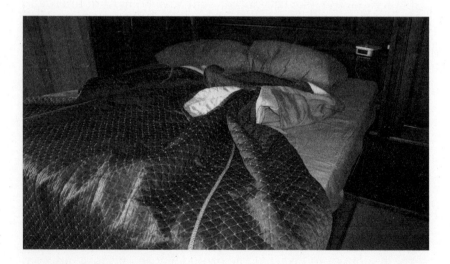

1) You made the bed.

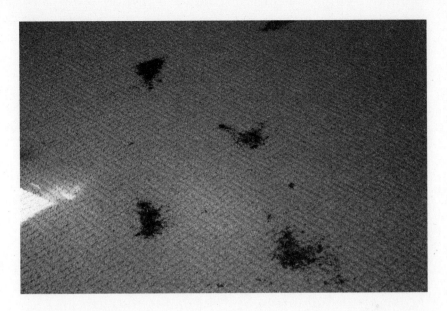

2) You walked the dog, and then came into the house with your shoes on.

3) You didn't wash your hands before lunch.

4) Or before lifting the seat.

5) You cleaned your SeaDoo Flame Arrestor on the kitchen table. Using her toothbrush.

HOW GOOD IS GOOD ENOUGH?

As you continue to work on your relationship to make it more satisfactory for both of you, you will eventually realize that you and your wife have different standards for almost everything. Sometimes these standards are so far apart that there's no overlap between you, which makes it impossible to find compatibility through seeking common ground. Do the following evaluation exercise with your wife. You circle your answers, and let her circle hers. This will give each of you a heads-up as to where change needs to occur for the two of you to find everlasting peace and eternal happiness.

1) How do you dress for a night out?

WOMAN'S ANSWERS:
a) New clothes
b) Designer outfit
c) Clean dress
d) Jogging suit

MAN'S ANSWERS:
a) New pants
b) Clean and ironed pants
c) Clean pants
d) Pants

2) Where do you like to sit at a restaurant?

WOMAN'S ANSWERS:
a) Away from the door
b) Away from the bright lights
c) Away from the kitchen
d) Away from the restaurant

MAN'S ANSWERS:

a) Beside the peanut barrel
b) At the bar
c) Near the rear exit
d) In my car

3) What do you look for in a car?

WOMAN'S ANSWERS:

a) Clean and pretty
b) Simple to drive
c) Big mirrors
d) Quiet

MAN'S ANSWERS:

a) Big engine
b) Mean-looking
c) Lean and low
d) Loud exhaust

4) What are the factors that make an enjoyable dinner at home?

WOMAN'S ANSWERS:

a) Balance of flavours and colours
b) Continuity from appetizer through entrée and then dessert
c) Leisurely pace of serving and eating
d) Candlelight

MAN'S ANSWERS:

a) Delivered on time
b) Extra cheesebread
c) No tip expected
d) Leftovers

5) What mood do you need to be in to be interested in sex?

WOMAN'S ANSWERS:
a) Relaxed
b) In love with my partner
c) Confident in our relationship
d) Having a sense of well-being

MAN'S ANSWERS:
a) Awake
b) Sober
c) Indoors
d) Not alone

NEVER BE EFFORTLESS

Men are programmed to be results-oriented. It's our historic duty to go out in the wilderness, track down a wild beast, kill it and bring it home for the family to eat. Nobody wants to hear "I gave it 110 per cent but it didn't go well, so instead we're all going to be vegetarians." But the shocking truth is that results aren't nearly as important to women as they are to men.

Yes, women like good results and they're very pleased when you actually do something, but their prime focus is on the amount of effort you put into the task. Particularly if it's a task you're doing for *them*. They equate your amount of effort with the amount of value you put on them and your relationship.

So when you get your wife a really lame birthday gift, it's not just the psychedelic, battery-operated, talking foot massager that upsets her, it's the inference that you gave the whole process a minimum of thought and interest. And that feeling is in no way enhanced by the fact that you bought it from a guy at work who had previously purchased it as a gift for *his* wife.

Same thing with household chores. When she asks you to make the bed, she's not expecting you to just pile everything in the middle of the mattress and then throw a duvet over it. When she asks you to help scrub the pots and pans, she doesn't want to see you fire up the gas power washer. Even if you do the work when she's not there, your wife has an innate ability to look at the results and be able to judge within four ergs how much energy was required to do the job in question.

She will notice that you cut the lawn, but she'll be more aware of how you didn't trim around any of the trees so that, looking down from the second story, they resemble Mitch Miller smoking a cigar. She'll notice that you washed the car, but she'll see the tires and windows aren't done and the fast-food bags are still piled up on the dashboard.

Now, I know you might say that she should appreciate the things you do rather than criticize the things you don't do, but the problem is there are so few things in the first category and so many in the second. And the only way to make the two balance is through time and effort. More specifically, *your* time and effort. If you do a bad job on the lawn but it takes you all day, that's a lot more acceptable to her than coming home, seeing the lawn and finding you lying on the couch, watching a football game that you recorded last year.

The root of the problem is that women look for meaning in everything—the complete opposite of what men do. So when you make very little effort, to your wife that means her wants are of very little importance to you. That's not good, because she will eventually reciprocate in a way that makes lawn mowing seem like a privilege.

My advice is to always put in the time and effort. Even if you give your wife a four-carat diamond ring for her birthday, she will . . . okay, that's a bad example. But even if you do something great for your wife, if it comes too easily for you, she will not appreciate it as much as when you make an effort.

This is the scourge of the rich, that the husbands can always take the easy route of buying something expensive or having their staff send over a thousand roses or whatever. While their wives enjoy being showered with gifts in the short run, over the long haul they want to see a level of effort. The more you try, the more you care. And if you don't care enough to try, she will eventually not try enough to care.

GENDER TREND

I'm going to ask you to try to go back in time to when you were about nine years old and had a list of heroes that included sports stars, television stars, movie stars and fast-food mascots. You wanted to be like them in every way possible. However, if you were four feet tall and white, being exactly like Shaquille O'Neal was a challenge, so instead you associated yourself through clothes and style.

You got the Nike shoes and the Elvis haircut and the Elton John glasses and the Jerry Lee Lewis mood ring. This was your way of being one of the gang. Of being accepted. At the time, you thought it was the coolest thing ever to have the same jersey as Michael Jordan, but over the years you came to regard this behaviour as allowing yourself to be manipulated by the world's craftiest marketers.

It was at that point that you began to disconnect from trends and fads and generally whatever was popular. Instead, you found things you were generally comfortable with—shoes, clothes, hairstyles, attitudes, thoughts and words.

Unfortunately, very few women go through this same transition. As young girls, they don't see imitation as a fad or a trend;

they see it as a sign of their commitment to renewing themselves continually throughout their lives, using any current changes as the catalyst for the process. You don't have enough energy or interest to renew yourself. It's all you can do to keep the old model of yourself running and roadworthy.

A Justin Bieber haircut ain't gonna help anybody. But if you're married to a woman who wants to stay relatively current with fashion and lifestyle changes, you'll be faced with three options.

One: you can hold your ground and try to bring your wife down to your level. It won't be easy, but if you stick with it, you may eventually get her to settle on old clothes she likes and a hairstyle and colour that are sustainable and to maintain unchanging opinions on everything despite overwhelming evidence to the contrary. The downside here is she will get as hard to look at as you are. And eventually, you will both stop looking.

Two: you can hold your ground on your own personal appearance and demeanour, but allow her the budget and freedom to keep up with the times in any way she sees fit. For much of the time, the two of you will have separate lives. She'll be a smart-looking, well-put-together modern woman drinking lattes and going to Pilates classes. And you'll be Homer Simpson. It's fine when you're apart, but when you go out to a social event together, she'll look perfect and you'll look like you're there to fix the fridge. Or maybe empty the fridge.

Three: you go her way, keeping up with the latest styles and trends in everything. Dye your hair orange, get your ears pierced, shave your back and wear a thong. Wear Italian shoes and shiny suits, fake a French accent and drive a Benz. Even if it's an '81.

But here's your best option: plan your social calendar a year in advance and identify the dates where you will be going somewhere with your wife where it's important for you to look like you've been out of the house in the last ten years. Circle those. A week before each, check the latest fashion trends and get yourself the absolute most conservative version of whatever is popular.

That's your zone, but you should go into it just long enough to survive the event, then return to your default mode with the too-small jeans and the "She's with Stupid" T-shirt. That way your wife's not embarrassed when she's out with you and you're not embarrassed when she's not.

MORE THINGS TO THINK ABOUT WHILE STILL WAITING FOR YOUR WIFE

- I fear no man, but most women scare the crap out of me.
- My life seems to go better when I keep checking to make sure my wife is smiling.
- It is easier for a camel to go through the eye of a needle than for a woman to go through a mall.
- There are three ways of explaining to your wife why you didn't call—none of them work.
- Your wife will still have bad-hair days, even when you don't even have hair days.
- Just because women are cute and petite doesn't mean they're harmless. They're sort of like pink hand grenades.
- It's okay to have lots of women in your life as long as you have them one at a time.
- For a person with a tiny waist, she sure has a lot of guts.
- A wife will sometimes want someone to tell her what to do, but it had better not be her husband.
- A trashy woman is like the Tilt-A-Whirl. You don't want to be on it for the rest of your life, but it's a great, quick ride that makes your head spin and money fall out of your pants.
- When you've been dating a woman for a while, you'll be able to take her out any time you want, but after

you've been married for a while, she'll be able to take <u>you</u> out any time <u>she</u> wants.

· I never completely understood the story of Adam and Eve, but it does explain why most men really like ribs.

· On average, single men enjoy the sound of a woman's voice more than married men do.

THE BAG OF TRICKS

When you've been dating a girl for a while, you get some sense of what you're dealing with, but only after you get married—or at least live together—do you begin to experience how complex life becomes when one of the partners is carrying most of the equipment for that life in her purse.

At its best, a purse is a blessing—an attractive accessory that enhances the look and style of the wearer, while simultaneously providing quick, systematic access to a vast assortment of essentials. Sadly, the purse I've just described is a myth. The purses that are being used here on earth, by earth women, are not a blessing, they are a curse. They don't mean to be, and they're certainly not designed to be. It just happens.

It happens because of compromise—the *wrong* compromise. Let me explain. It starts with women not liking bulgy things. They want to have a sleek, smooth look. They don't want to see things bulging out anywhere. I have some male friends who think women enjoy seeing a bulge in a man's pants, but I say if that's true, they're looking for his wallet. So because they don't like bulges, if their clothes had pockets they wouldn't put anything in them anyway. Most of them find even empty pockets too bulgy.

So the first condition is that, unlike men, women don't like to carry things inside their clothing. That is, unfortunately, in direct conflict with the second condition, which is that you absolutely have to carry things—credit cards, cash, driver's licence, car keys, hand gun, etc. So right away a purse becomes a necessity.

And it happens early in life. You'll see nine- and ten-year-old girls carrying a purse. This is actually the source of the real problems, because at that age they don't need to carry much, so they can focus on the style. They will pick out some great-looking purse that will look fashionable because it goes so well with their hairstyle and their braces. It will become their favourite purse. They will remember it their entire lives. Even through high school, the purse can remain predominantly a fashion accessory because it's mainly carrying money and makeup. The problems start when they graduate and get a job and then a husband and then a family.

Fishermen have different equipment for fly-fishing, lake fishing, drift fishing and deep-sea fishing. They don't do it all out of the same tackle box. Women soon realize they can't do it all out of the same purse. They can't carry the papers for work and the shopping lists and the coupons and the handi-wipes and the pens and the makeup and the retainer and the shoehorn and the paperback and the receipts from everything they've bought in the last five years all inside that one little, attractive purse.

So now we add the third condition, which is the decision to buy a purse that is better suited to the application. I'm talking about a big purse. I'm talking about a big, ugly purse. This is like a backpack without the metal frame. It has compartments and dividers and layers and four or five entrances. Once a woman has that purse and organizes it properly, she is ready for World War III. And everyone is happy. For a few days.

But then she'll catch a glimpse of that purse in the mirror as it hangs on her shoulder or she'll see it lying on the counter and spilling over into a chair. Someone will take her picture while she's holding that purse and it will make her look fat. Then one day she will line up her purses, from the smallest, most chic to the hugest, most grotesque and she will realize that she has to make a compromise.

One choice, the first compromise, is to discount style and just carry on with the big, ugly thing 'cause it's working. This is a tough one because she's already doing it with her marriage.

The second compromise is to carry a medium-sized, somewhat stylish purse and carry the bare minimum of essentials in it. To her, this is the worst solution because it acknowledges that the big one is too ugly to use, but it subliminally suggests that she's not worthy of the small, stylish purse she really wants. In her mind, she'd be pretending to be royalty when, in fact, she is staff.

The third compromise is to carry that elegant little purse she loves and just live with the fact that you can't put anything in it. Not the wisest choice, but certainly understandable.

However, that's not the one she chooses. She opts for the worst compromise, which is to have the smallest purse and then ignore all of the laws of physics by packing it to the gills, like a cheap suitcase—sit on it, step on it, whatever you gotta do. As long as it looks good.

If this sounds like your wife, just let it go. Smile and give her a kiss on the cheek. Just don't rub up against her purse. It might explode and somebody could lose an eye.

THE SILENT TRUCE

For the first ten years of your marriage, you will each be on a mission to change the other person in a way that will make them more like you. The women are very direct about it because they feel, and rightfully so, that they have more work to do and also have the upper hand. They will express their wishes verbally at sufficient volume or higher, and on a fairly regular basis. They will also not shrug it off, or leave it for another day, or get over it.

Men tend to be more casual. In this context, *casual* means "cowardly." A man will rarely confront his wife about anything.

He's seen the resultant cyclone before and is not sure his personal aircraft has enough fuel or structural integrity to fly through it. So he mainly mumbles to himself and secretly wishes that she would magically morph into the woman he fantasized she was when he bought the ring.

If he feels like he has a legitimate criticism, he doesn't have the nerve to confront her directly, but will use it as grist for his snide comments in front of her in the company of friends at a social function. This rarely brings him the desired results. In this context, *rarely* means "never."

In fact, with few exceptions, neither of these approaches works. You may think you can change another adult human being, but to pull it off, you need to overpower twenty-five years of permissive upbringing and two million years of evolution. You may change them for an evening, or a couple of days, or a week, or maybe even a whole month, but eventually they will return to their default position.

It's like gravity: it's pulling you when you're not even thinking about it. So when each of you realizes you're not going to be able to change the other, and yet you still want to stay together, you need to make a different arrangement. And you do. And you don't ever discuss it or even suggest it exists. It's like cleavage—you're aware of it but don't dare say anything in case it disappears.

That arrangement is a silent truce. It's a device that each of you uses to satisfy yourselves that you are being treated fairly in this relationship. If you see a hundred pairs of shoes in your wife's closet, you get yourself a dirt bike. If she sees a couple of cases of beer in the back of your truck, she picks up a box of expensive chocolates. If she gets to watch *Dancing with the Stars* on Friday night, it means you get to watch WWE on Saturday night. If she knows you've been to a strip club, she doesn't have a conniption. She goes out and gets her hair and nails done. And then has a conniption.

This is all nature's way of helping couples get along. You were hoping to change the other person so that you could do what you wanted. That's never going to happen, so instead you have a system where the other person does what they want and, to get even, you get to do what you want.

Revenge is much easier than compromise. But the key is that neither of you can ever reveal that you are aware of the arrangement. You have to remain oblivious. Shouldn't be a problem.

THE GREAT DIVIDE

There is no activity that more clearly defines the difference between men and women than shopping. Women can shop with their friends for twelve hours straight, come home with nothing and call that a great day. The only thing men hate worse than going shopping and not buying anything is being dragged out shopping with a buddy who doesn't buy anything.

That's because of another basic difference between men and women. When a woman sees something she likes, she thinks, "I like that." When a man sees something he likes, he thinks, "I'm getting that."

Women are passive shoppers. They're allowed to just enjoy the experience. Not men. They're aggressive shoppers. Their job is to get stuff. If they see something they like and then don't get it, that's a blow to their masculinity. If you liked it, why didn't you get it? Couldn't you afford it? Did you chicken out? Weren't you man enough to get it?

Every time a man goes shopping with his wife and comes home with nothing, his ego shrinks a bit. It's no better when he goes alone. That's one of the reasons a man will never go shopping until he's ready to buy. If I were a sales clerk, I would focus on the men. They're not fooling around. They're there to establish their masculinity by buying something. To a salesman, it's like shooting fish in a barrel.

And that goes way back. We're supposed to be hunters. A man who goes shopping and comes home empty-handed is either bad at picking hunting grounds or a lousy shot. It's embarrassing for men to shop and not buy. That's what catalogues are for. Or the Internet. Where we can embarrass ourselves in the privacy of our own homes. Once we're out in the store, we're dealing with a salesperson who, no matter what excuse we give, is going to assume that if we don't buy it's because we're not really men.

Most men would rather buy something they don't want and don't need than come home empty-handed. Women are just the opposite. They think not buying makes them seem more aloof and harder to get. Men aren't hard to get and don't even know how to fake it.

When women are looking to make a purchase, they put most of their time and energy into looking at all the options and getting the best possible deal, and then they do the buying. Men just buy the thing right away and then put all their time and energy into making it look like a good purchase.

Neither is wrong, they're just different. They can't work together, but they can work in tandem. It's better if the woman does the research and the shopping but doesn't bring the man into the mix until they're ready to buy. The woman gets the value she's looking for, the man gets the sense of accomplishment. Everybody wins.

THERE'S SOMETHING FUNNY GOING ON

A lot of the reason I wrote this book is to help open your eyes to the thoughts and actions that are hurting your chances of having a successful relationship with the woman in your life. We all know that if people were all the same, it would make them far less interesting. But there are differences in people that make cohabitation difficult. Some of these differences are obvious, and they're easier to deal with.

One of you needs to change. And I'm pretty sure it's you.

But other differences are more subtle. You may not even be aware of them, which makes them even more dangerous because if you don't see them, you won't see a reason to change them. One of the most destructive differences between men and women is what they find funny. Women like clever wit and sophisticated repartee. Men like slapstick and bathroom jokes. If men get a whiff of a bad odour, they will take a really deep breath that almost kills them and then laugh about how bad that smells.

Men love jokes in general and often use them as a substitute for conversation. Women prefer funny stories to jokes. They want to know about the characters in the story and the emotional turmoil they're in. Men just want the punchline.

So if you're going to get up at a party and tell your favourite joke about the priest, the nun and the unicorn, you're better off to just tell it to the men, even if you have to tell it to them one at a time. If you insist on including the women, you need to rework the joke into the form of a story. You can try to keep all the funny stuff, but you need to add a lot of narrative and romance and you need to make it a personal story. But don't pretend to be the nun.

As a general rule, don't tell jokes to women unless you're Ellen DeGeneres. In fact, trying to make a woman laugh at all is a dangerous game. That's because when you try to make a woman laugh, you are revealing what you yourself find funny. That will usually hurt you. As a man, you think it's hilarious that your buddy's pig fell down the well. But when you try to tell your wife about it, she will be horrified. Partially because she will be so sympathetic to this poor, helpless animal having a horrible accident, but mainly because you're laughing so hard you've got tears in your eyes and can barely get the story out.

I'm not advising you not to tell funny stories to women, but I *am* saying you need to look at the subject of the story and assess its potential for getting those laughs you so desperately need. Generally, stories where bad things happen to animals have a very high failure rate.

Similarly, when people get hurt, women don't find that nearly as funny as you do. Seeing a nerdy guy going down the street reading a science book and walking right into a telephone pole may be hilarious to you, but a woman is more likely to run over and console him. And when she has him feeling better, she'll return and make you feel worse.

I'm not sure why men find personal injury so funny. Maybe it's our competitive nature. Somebody falling makes us feel better. Maybe we empathize—we hurt ourselves on a regular basis and it's comforting to know we're not the only ones. Maybe we just find any surprise funny, good or bad. Whatever the reason, nothing hurts your relationship more than laughing at something she doesn't think is funny.

There is a solution, but it comes in two parts. Part one: spend a few hours a week with your buddies—at work, on a sports team, at the Lodge, whatever. This is your laugh time. You can tell your jokes and they can tell theirs. You can laugh at each other getting hurt and then toss a pig down a well. Get it all out of your system.

Part two: the rest of the time you will be with your wife. Do not tell any jokes or funny stories. If somebody says something or does something or some innocent person or animal gets hurt in some ridiculous way, do not laugh. Instead, focus on your wife and do whatever she does. Be sympathetic, be offended—whatever she does, you do. If she laughs, then and only then can you laugh. Don't ever laugh first or you'll be playing with fire.

Throughout the history of successful marriages, you would have heard "I'm going out with my wife for a romantic dinner" or "I'm going out with my wife to shop for new furniture," but you would never hear "I'm going out with my wife for a few laughs."

BEING CONSISTENTLY INCONSISTENT

You've probably heard throughout your life that everybody is looking for a partner who is consistent. Someone they can rely on. Someone who's the same person today as they were yesterday and will be tomorrow.

Well, okay, I guess it's a nice theory and it works well in romantic novels. Unfortunately, very few of us live in romantic novels. You're more likely to find us in washing machine manuals—we get soaked, we get agitated, we get spun out of control and at the end of the day, we tumble into a hamper.

And in that environment, being consistent is not the best way to go. It is impossible for a man who's consistent to have both a wife and friends. If he's always the same guy, if he talks and acts the same way when he's with his wife as he does when he's with his friends, that will not work. If he treats his wife like his friends, she'll think he's a jerk. If he treats his friends like his wife, they'll think he's a wuss. If he tries to compromise by finding the small overlap of personalities between his wife and his friends and then restricting all of his conversation and activities to fall within that tight framework, they will find him boring and he will be exhausted and have a headache all the time.

So don't do it. The truth is nobody cares if you're the same with your wife as you are with your friends. Your friends don't care how you are with your wife. They know how they are with *their* wives and they'd rather just have kind of an unspoken agreement that it's something nobody ever talks about.

Conversely, your wife may be concerned about how you are with your friends, so the secret there is to never have your wife and your friends in the same room. The friends won't mind, and if your wife ever does meet them, she probably won't mind never seeing them again.

The problem is, your friends and your wife want entirely different things from you. Your friends want you be a light, fun-loving guy who will go along with whatever the gang has decided to do and, when necessary, will give the exact same story to the cops, word for word. Your wife, on the other hand, wants you to be the perfect, caring, considerate husband, deferring to her and supporting her in all she does. Your friends don't wanna know about that crap. If you don't believe me, try telling your friends about some really nice thing you did for your wife and watch the reaction. I'm talking eye-rolling and gagging surrounding a barrage of unflattering comments loaded heavily with sarcasm and disbelief.

So don't make the mistake of being consistent—being the same guy all the time. Instead, you need to be consistently inconsistent. If you're Guy A with your wife, sure, you need to be Guy A every time you're with your wife. But you need to be Guy B with your friends. And Guy C with your boss. And Guy D with the policeman who is currently going through the contents of your trunk.

Shakespeare said that all the world's a stage. And it's a stage we're all going through. You're in a play, but you never play yourself. Instead, you have all these characters you play, and every time they make an entrance, they need to be the same character they were three scenes ago. The trick is to never have two of your characters in any one scene. I suggest you limit the cast to yourself, your wife and a few friends. Don't even think about having another woman in the wings. You're not that good an actor.

ALL IN THE GAME

It's perfectly natural that whenever you have two people spending a lot of time together, it creates a certain level of competition. Each person has a vague idea of where they stand in certain aspects of the relationship, but they need to have that confirmed. Which one is smarter? More fit? Harder working? More successful? Etc., etc. The problem is that a full-blown overt competition between a husband and wife on the daily issues of career, finance and family will lead to bad feelings.

So instead, you need to focus the natural competition on a fun parlour game. Maybe checkers or Trivial Pursuit or Monopoly. You should play these games with your wife to establish where the supremacy lies. You could even just play cards. If your wife is good at math, you could play cribbage. If your wife is bad at math, you could play cribbage and have a chance of winning. But I wouldn't recommend it.

My advice is to play hard, but lose. And be a gracious loser. Compliment your wife on her expertise and ability. Make her cajole you into playing these games and then continue to lose. Let her feel the great pride that comes from being a winner. It will put a spring in her step. She'll feel good about herself and be sympathetic to you. But most important, she will expect more from herself and less from you.

You can cheer her on as she climbs the corporate ladder. You can tell everyone that she makes way more money than you do. And make sure she's there when you say it. Then give her a kiss. She's a winner and you're not. You've been forced to play a supporting role in the marriage. While she's away at conventions or annual board meetings, you're fishing with your buddies or going to football games. While she's stressing over the pressures of mergers and acquisitions, you're deep-frying a wild turkey in the back of your pickup truck.

And be sure to keep reminding her of how proud you are. Keep the praise coming or she could suddenly be jealous of you. And when she does finally get a minute of free time, whip out that cribbage board and let her trounce you again. A painful reminder of which one's the champ and which one's the chump. And pretend to be a little upset when you lose. Tell her she's so lucky to be the smart one. Meanwhile, you're so smart to be the lucky one.

YOU'RE AN IDIOT

At some point in your marriage, your wife is going to turn to you and exclaim, "You're an idiot!"

Now, you may be sensitive enough to take this as a hurtful criticism, but if you'll just pause for a minute and take the long view, this could be one of the best days of your life. But before we get to that, we need to examine the details surrounding the accusation.

Let's start with the exact wording. Was it simply "You're an idiot!" or were adjectives added, as in "You're a complete idiot!" or "You're a total idiot!" or the always popular "You're a stupid idiot!" (With this last one, you have the option of pointing out the redundancy of the word *stupid* since there's no such thing as a smart idiot, although I wouldn't recommend doing so unless you enjoy eating at drive-thrus and sleeping in your car.)

While it's true that adding adjectives emphasizes the message, it doesn't necessarily make it more negative. However, if the letter *F* is heavily involved in said adjective, that's not a good sign. For our purposes, let's assume that the wording is more on the mild side and implies some opportunity for reconciliation.

Now we have to look at the tone. Let's start with the pitch and amplitude. If it was below 50 decibels, it's almost a compliment. If it's over 110 decibels, you've got a problem. And what were the physical dynamics when the sentence was said? Were you both sitting? Was she standing? Was she standing on the kitchen table? Although you may feel hurt and rejected, this whole incident can work in your favour.

The first step is to not overreact. In fact, don't react at all. Just take it all in and think about it. Go beyond the words and try to determine her inference. Did she say "You're an idiot!" like it was a total surprise to her? Or did she say it as though she had suspected it all along?

This second situation is the one you want. If your idiocy was a surprise to her, you're going to have to continue being an idiot until she lowers her expectations. When a wife thinks her husband is smart and competent, every time he does something dumb or incompetent she takes it as a personal insult. She feels he has the brains and ability to do things properly but didn't because he doesn't care enough about her. It may not be true, but if that's how your wife feels about it, the truth is irrelevant. On the other hand, once she has you recalibrated as a useless idiot, anything you do that's not half-bad will be greatly appreciated.

However, the moment your wife accepts that you're an idiot is the moment you have to stop being one. That's because there is a very narrow range of idiocy your wife will accept. If you overshoot the mark, your wife will wonder why she married you and it will negatively affect her opinion of herself, which will be your fault and will put the marriage in jeopardy. On the other hand, if you're not idiotic enough, she will raise the bar. So to keep the perfect balance, you have the choice of either being a smart person who occasionally does idiotic things, or an idiot who occasionally does smart things. I recommend the latter.

As we get older, our memory starts to fade and with the second option, you would forget to do the smart things, which won't hurt you, but if you choose the first option you will forget to do the stupid things, which will prevent you from being an idiot, which is idiotic.

So when your wife says "You're an idiot!" look hurt and hide your gratitude while you silently give yourself an "attaboy."

MAKING YOUR MOVE

Whenever you want to do something that you know your wife does not want you to do, you have to stop and think. In the early years of marriage, you will probably just go ahead and do it on the basis that you'll have more luck begging for forgiveness than asking for permission. But, as I'll explain in another section of this book, acquiring lasting forgiveness from your significant other is a fool's game with life-changing consequences. So I recommend the "asking permission" route. In fact, I'd even suggest you try to get her to give her your blessing in the activity.

Sound impossible? Not to an experienced husband, or "lifer," as they're known in the business.

To achieve this seemingly impossible result will require a certain amount of gamesmanship on your part. And not just any gamesmanship: I'm talking about the kind of subtle strategy used by master chess players. I'll use a chess game as an analogy for two reasons. First, because it's the closest physical representation of the "bait and switch" approach so necessary to successful negotiation, and second, because I wanted to show you that I know the word *analogy*.

Let's say you want to spend this coming Saturday fishing with your friend Ted. Your wife, on the other hand, wants you to go shopping with her to get a new washing machine. So this is how it looks at the start of your chess game.

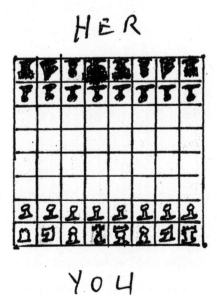

HER

YOU

You have the first move. You mention that Ted asked you to go fishing on Saturday but you told him you can't because the two of you are going shopping for a washer. Chess equivalent: King's Pawn to King 3.

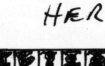

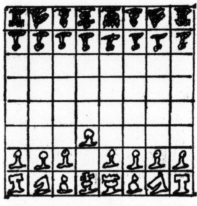

Her move. She answers, "That's right. Maybe you can go with Ted another time. We'll see." Chess equivalent: King's Pawn to King 4.

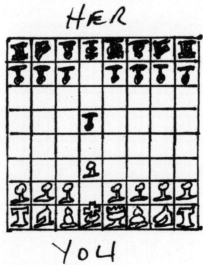

You mention that you've been researching washers, and as environmentally responsible adults, you think you should buy a high-efficiency unit that uses much less water and detergent. Chess equivalent: King's Bishop to Queen's Bishop 4.

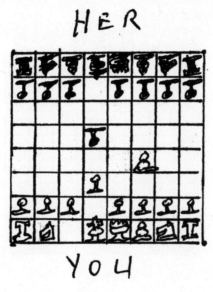

She agrees and compliments you on your opinion. Chess equivalent: Queen's Pawn to Queen 3. (She wanted to go to Queen 4, but your bishop prevents that.)

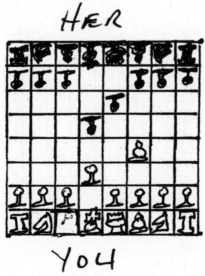

Your move. You say how glad you are that she feels the same way. The high-efficiency units start at around $1,500 which means you'll have to cut back in other areas, but we all have to be prepared to sacrifice to save the planet. Chess equivalent: Queen to King's Rook 5.

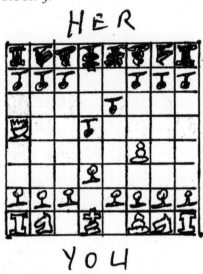

"Fifteen hundred dollars?! Wow. That's a lot of money. Maybe we should think it over." Chess equivalent: King's Knight to King's Bishop 3 (putting your queen at risk).

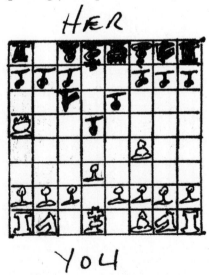

Your move. The phone rings. Your wife answers. It's Ted's wife, asking her to spend Saturday at the spa since Ted is going fishing. She comes off the phone and announces a change of plans and hopes you have a great time with Ted on Saturday. She never needs to know that you arranged the phone call. Chess equivalent: Queen to King's Bishop 7, taking her pawn. Checkmate.

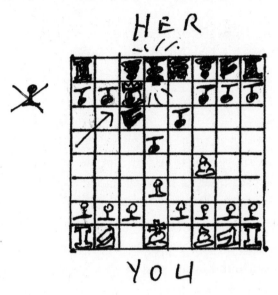

FORGIVE AND FORGET? FORGET IT

I've heard that there are people in this world who can forgive and forget, who can bury the hatchet, who can let bygones be bygones, but I can't honestly say I've ever met any of them. Most people pretend to forgive, but they never forget, and even if they bury the hatchet it's in a very shallow grave. For them, bygones are "are heres." There are two main reasons for that: 1) normal people aren't that nice and 2) we are instinctively programmed neither to forgive nor forget. It has to do with survival.

It's important that you learn from anything that doesn't kill you. So if somebody does something that hurts you, if you can forgive and forget, you're no further ahead.

Rather than be upset with someone who won't forgive and forget, I suggest you look at the reality of the situation. You did something wrong or dangerous or both and put that person at risk, so when you ask them to forgive and forget, you're asking them to put themselves at risk again, and this time, with a person who's already proven themselves to be unreliable. So basically, you're asking them to be an idiot. And you're offended when they refuse.

Of course, all of this is a precursor to what I really want to talk about, which is that—and please pay attention here—your wife will *never* forgive and forget. Let me rephrase that: she will *never* forgive. She may forget what happened specifically, but she knows better than to forgive, even if she can't remember what it is she's not forgiving you for.

I've heard stories about couples who've been married for over twenty-five years and in the heat of an argument she will bring up hurtful things that he did or said between their first and second dates. I'm telling you this not as a criticism of women. Quite the opposite. I'm telling you that women are more suited for survival. The ability to forgive and forget has caused a lot of injuries and may be the reason so many animals are extinct. If, instead of forgiving and forgetting a harsh winter, they used their anger and memory to move to a warmer climate, they might still be with us.

So before you do something that you know is going to cause problems at home, you need to accept that whatever the fallout is, it will go on forever. I've heard husbands in that situation say, "She'll get over it," and yes she will, but that's not the point. She'll make sure *you'll* never get over it. Thirty-five years later, when you do something completely unrelated or make a comment that in no way refers to what we'll call "the incident," she will throw it back onto the table like it happened an hour ago.

You are married to a queen. When you please her, her favour will smile on you for a day or so. When you displease her, a part of you will be banished for all of eternity. It's her way of trying to make you a better man. I know how annoying that is for you.

BLUE BOOK VALUE

If you've ever been in a position where you suddenly have a vehicle to sell, either because you bought another car or you've had a financial setback or the vehicle in question is on fire, you will soon become uncomfortably aware of what they call "blue book value."

This is supposed to be an objective market valuation of your vehicle given its age, mileage and condition. It's usually good news for the buyer and bad news for the seller. I'm not sure how the blue book concept got started, but my suspicions are that sellers had unrealistic ideas of what their cars were worth. It's hard to believe that a vehicle you still owe ten thousand dollars on is valued at seven hundred bucks.

The whole premise of the market-value approach is to educate both parties so that mistakes made by the seller do not get transferred on to an unsuspecting buyer. It's really a way to clean up the used car business, which, up until about twenty years ago, really needed it.

Personally, I've had both positive and negative experiences from this approach, but overall I'd say it's good to have a consistent, reliable way of measuring what a vehicle is worth. The truth is we sometimes need a wake-up call, a reminder of the true value of things. It's an outside-in approach that doesn't come naturally to many of us. And I'm saying that it's a worthwhile exercise, not just for our possessions, but for *ourselves*.

Maybe at this point you've been married for fifteen years or more and you have a conception about which one of you has retained their appeal in the open free market. It's important that you find out the facts. You need to see the blue book value of both yourself and your wife. Chances are you think she's lost a lot of value since you took her off the lot, while you, on the other hand, have retained, if not increased, your original sticker price. You need to find out if all of that is true because, in time, your perception of those relative values will impact your relationship.

Here's what to do. Ask your wife to meet you at a busy restaurant for dinner at six o'clock. Tell her you're pretty sure you can be there by six, but just in case, she should just go to the bar and wait for you if you're not there. You arrive at the restaurant at 5:45, but sit near the back in a dark corner where nobody can see you, but you can see the bar. You'll see your wife come in and look around for you and then sit at the bar and wait. Watch what happens.

Do men speak to her? Do they offer to buy her a drink? Pay no attention to her response. It's irrelevant and will only hurt your feelings. You need to focus on what the men are doing. Are they trying to include her in their conversation? Are they moving closer? When you've seen enough, slip out the back door and then re-enter the restaurant and have a big, juicy hello and be damn glad she's with you.

And what's even more important, you need to return to the same restaurant a few days later by yourself. Sit at the bar and try to make conversation with women who are alone, as your wife was. You need to focus on the women's response. Do they try to engage in a conversation? Or do they pretend someone they knew just drove by on a motorcycle and then rush out to chase them?

Now, don't get me wrong: this is not an exercise to show you how disappointing your blue book value is. It's to make you thankful that you're not for sale.

A BETTER MAN

Who can forget Jack Nicholson's classic line from *As Good As It Gets:* "You make me want to be a better man"? This could be the most dangerous sentence ever said by a man out loud. The reason it's so diabolical is that it's the sentence women most want to hear, and it's also the sentence men least want to say.

Women want to hear it because they see their man as a project, a work in progress. They know he will change and they accept that. But if they do nothing he may change for the worse. So if they try to make him better, he will at least remain somewhat the same. Men, on the other hand, don't want anybody or anything to change. It confuses them. They want their wives to look and act exactly the same as the day they met them. Regardless of anything the man might do to negatively influence the woman's appearance, behaviour or attitude. Especially attitude.

Men reject change. Expecting, wanting or forcing him to change works in direct opposition to his misguided instincts. And even if a guy wants to be a better man, that doesn't necessarily make things better. That's because a husband's idea of what a better man is will probably be a lot different than his wife's. A man thinks a better man is more manly. Just like him, only more so. Bigger, stronger, more assertive, more aggressive, with more testosterone. Whereas his wife thinks to be a better man he needs to be more feminine. Kinder, gentler, more caring, more sensitive, with more estrogen.

For me, the basis of any disagreement between men and women is expressed when they stand face to face and ask each other, "Why can't you be more like me?" When a man and woman are similar, all of the problems go away. However, they are also an incredibly boring couple and run the risk of being murdered by their friends. That's because nature thrives on difference. It needs opposing forces to survive. From the fertilization of seeds to the orbits of the planets, it's opposing forces that make it all work.

So here we are in an environment defined by our need to be different, trying to fulfill an innate desire for the other person to be the same. There's no hope for peace, but maybe we can reach a truce. If each partner tries to be like the other while simultaneously accepting each other's need to be different, throw in a little alcohol once in a while and maybe we can make this thing work.

THE KINETIC CONNECTION

Whenever I see a car sitting in a driveway with a big pink bow stuck on the windshield, I immediately start worrying about the guy who bought it. That's because this is wrong on oh, so many levels.

He's obviously bought this vehicle as a surprise for his wife. Okay, first question: Why would he buy her something that expensive? Is it love? Maybe. Is it guilt? Now you're talking.

And why would he buy her something that expensive and then make it a surprise? Because he thinks she would really like a fully loaded Rambler American convertible? No. He's not thinking at all. He's assuming. He's taking what he would like and projecting that onto his wife.

That's how he got into trouble in the first place. The odds are pretty good that his wife is going to see this thing in the driveway and think bad thoughts. Like "This guy just spent a whole bunch of our money on something I don't even care about and he did it without discussing it with me and now we have no money to buy anything I would actually enjoy."

And to top it off, he's expecting her to squeal with excitement and hug and kiss him like he's somebody else. None of that is likely to happen. My guess is within an hour she'll be reading a book in a locked bedroom and he'll be trying to feed a large pink bow to a garbage disposal.

It's hard to know where to start on this issue, but let's go with the different attitudes on cars. Most men love cars. They name them. They personalize them. They see them as an extension of their personality and manhood. Whereas women see them as cars. A woman looks at a car the way a man looks at a stove. They have a purpose and some are better than others, but overall it's not something personal. And when you're getting a woman a gift, it should *always* be something personal.

To understand the difference in the way the two sexes look at cars, you have to examine the way they feel about any kind of movement. Men love movement. As kids, they love to watch wheels go around and see big trucks go down the road. As mature adults, they love to watch wheels go around and see big trucks go down the road. Similarly, men will sit and watch a construction site or a roofing job or water running out of a hose for hours on end.

Women don't do that. Women feel they need to be doing something. They need to accomplish something. Men feel that something needs to get done. Something needs to be accomplished. But they don't have to be the ones doing it. That's why they like to see really powerful, efficient machinery at work. Because it compensates for their inertness and raises the overall productivity level without them having to contribute. For a man, that is a sweet feeling.

I'm not suggesting you fight these differences or even try to change them. I'm saying you need to accept them and you need to acknowledge them when you're making a gift selection. Here's a bulletin: when you buy a gift for your wife, it doesn't matter how much *you* like it. Instead, try to study her for hints as to what she's interested in and would enjoy. If that requires more sensitivity than your skill level can handle, ask a friend for suggestions. A female friend.

Don't just buy a set of pneumatic tools that you've always had your eye on and then wrap a big pink bow around them.

THE MAGIC OF GPS

*E*arlier in this book, I described how you can make travelling more pleasant by customizing the passenger seat so it faces backwards. But maybe that's too much work for you, or there's some other negative component that we'd both rather not go into. So for you, I recommend a modern miracle that can make driving long distances with your wife a positive experience for all. Of course, I'm talking about a GPS.

Now, I'm not exactly sure how GPS works. I thought at first that it had some magical way of sensing exactly where it is at each second and can then not only relay that location to you, but also help you get where you want to go. I have found out since that the GPS is only capable of finding satellites, not locations. Satellites are easier to find because they don't move and you're not involved in any way with telling the GPS where those satellites are. Once it finds the satellites, the rest is just software. By comparing the various angles of the satellite signals it can figure out its own location and then stick that on a map for you to see.

Same deal when you punch in a location. The GPS is programmed with all the roads that will take you from your current coordinates to the destination's coordinates. It's impersonal and deadly accurate. The exact opposite of your wife—except for the deadly part.

So now you have in your car the one thing that kills all arguments: an expert. Somebody who knows what they're talking about. In your life, you're not going to meet many such people. And neither are they.

Your only obstacle is that your wife may not trust the GPS, or she may prefer to travel without using it. It's very important that you win this particular argument, even if you lose a hundred others. You need your wife to accept the GPS as a feature that makes for a safer, more efficient driving experience. You're going to get where you're going in the best possible way, and it removes from her the onus of navigating.

You've got all the evidence on your side, and let's hope and pray that's enough. Because the GPS not only eliminates arguments between the two of you, it also removes the possibility of taking some bizarre side trip to visit the Bee Museum. GPS is like a man: it needs to know where it is, it needs to know where it's going, and it needs to go there.

Once you have her convinced, it's very important which voice you select to give you directions. Make sure it's a woman's voice. She doesn't need another male voice in the car pretending he knows what he's doing. But don't choose just any female voice. For example, a woman with a French accent telling you what moves to make is not going to sit well with your better half. Find a woman's voice that's as close as possible to hers. And then just sit back and enjoy.

The GPS will be giving the orders, not your wife. And there's a huge difference. The GPS will say everything the same way—there are no tone issues. If you make a mistake, the GPS will just say "recalculating" rather than call you harsh names. The GPS will constantly update your expected arrival time so you'll know how long you have to be civil to each other.

And the best part is you'll never have to remember how you got anywhere, because while your wife is asleep in the back seat, the GPS will still be perky and capable of getting you home.

MASTERING THE EVASIVE ANSWER

As a man growing up in a world where expectations of excellence are placed upon you, it is absolutely natural to adopt a keen, competitive approach. Even if you can't be the best, as long as you can beat somebody, you won't be the worst.

While this competitiveness may be necessary and even desirable on the playing field or in the world of commerce, it has no place in a successful relationship. It is not in your best interest to beat your wife at anything, even if you could.

And yet there are some areas where you are so obviously superior, like arm-wrestling or belching, that she will notice if you let her win, and that's even worse. So what you need to do is to take competition out of the marriage before it begins.

The essence of competition is confrontation, so if you remove confrontation, you will eradicate competition. I'm not talking about physical confrontation. Very few women want to challenge men to a weightlifting contest or Indian leg wrestling. I'm talking about verbal confrontation. Competition springs from verbal confrontation, and verbal confrontation springs from disagreements. So if we can avoid disagreements, we will avoid confrontation and its corollary, competition.

However, avoiding disagreements is tricky. You will need to learn how to master the evasive answer. The only sure way to never have a point of view that offends your significant other is for her to be never completely sure of what your point of view is. It's not an easy talent to learn, but once you have it, you will have a happy marriage and a successful future in any career that requires public approval.

The process begins when your spouse asks you a question. You must instantly evaluate the question and assign it to the appropriate category. Is this a straight factual question, such as "Do you know where the scissors are?" If so, you can give a straightforward, concise answer. I recommend "No." Because most of the time you just *think* you know where the scissors are and you're better off saying no than sending her on a wild goose chase.

Or maybe the question has a hint of accusation in it—"Did you prune my roses?" Be careful. Notice the tone. Calling them "my roses" indicates extreme displeasure with the pruning job. And the fact that she's asking you means you're her prime suspect. If you've been lying to women for years and learned from your father, you may be able to just go with "Nope. Not me." If you want to take a shot at a lame answer, you could try, "No, I don't think so." Whaddya mean you don't think so? No man forgets a good rose trimming. Instead, I suggest you deflect the question with "Yeah, sure, you asked me to." Now she has to respond, which will take the focus off you and dissipate her anger. And when she says, "I did not, you idiot," you can counter with "Oh, sorry, I thought that was what you wanted."

The third type of question is one that asks for your opinion of her. For example, "What is it that you like about me?" Be very, very careful. I know you have a little voice urging you to say "Everything," but it is wrong. Terribly wrong. You may also be tempted to respond by naming a body part. Another huge mistake. The best answer, again, is one that turns it back to her: "What I like best about you is that you would care what I like at all. I love you . . . What's for dinner?" Pure gold.

The fourth and most dangerous type of question, and the one for which I have no advice, is the one asking you to defend yourself—like "How do you feel about having a vasectomy?" Especially if she just asked you where the scissors are.

FIND YOUR CRUISING SPEED

A marriage is a lot like an airplane. Not in the sense that you're strip-searched regularly and are trapped in a tiny space with old magazines and with bathrooms at the back, and you have to pay for extra baggage. (Okay, in marriage you also pay for extra baggage.)

I mean that, just like an airplane, every marriage has its ideal cruising speed. This is when you're going slow enough to steer around mountains and flying barbecue lids, but fast enough to remain airborne. And in that airplane, one of you is the pilot and the other one is the co-pilot.

Let's say your wife is the pilot. Because she is. So she's initiating all of the flight controls and you're reacting to those changes in a way that tries to maintain the status quo. It's not something that will come automatically or quickly, so you'll have to work at it over an extended period of time.

You'll have that time because it won't matter at first. When you're newlyweds it's okay for the engines to be running full throttle because you're trying to get the marriage off the ground. But once you've reached altitude, you'll both have happier lives if you can avoid the nine-thousand-foot climbs, especially if they're followed by *ten*-thousand-foot drops. Your wife has two controls at her disposal:

1) Her mood—the rudder that controls the flight direction.
2) Her energy—the main engine that controls the speed you get to wherever she's pointing the plane.

You, on the other hand, have to make do with an auxiliary engine and wing flaps. But before you can work any of your controls, you need to calculate your ideal direction and cruising speed. Let's start with direction. You will find that there are certain subjects and areas of discussion that elicit a negative reaction from your wife. Quite often these areas centre around something you've done in the past that has not been met with favour. These are not happy destinations for either of you. When you hear the expression "Don't go there," these are the places referred to.

You need to be able to adjust the course of the airplane away from those no-fly zones. Unfortunately, your wife has the rudder and all you have are wing flaps. The best approach is to work on minor changes in direction until you get back on course. If she's turning the plane hard to starboard, you lower the port wing flaps and the plane will either come around to a prettier place or take a lot longer to get to the ugly one.

If she brings up that time at the office party when you slow-danced with the new receptionist, laugh if off and tell her what a bad dancer she was and that the two of you should go out dancing more often.

After a few years of marriage, you'll know the range on the compass that contains the good destinations and you'll figure out how to move her towards those, one flap at a time.

On the energy issue, you will find that your marriage has an ideal cruising speed, where you're both contented, rather than ecstatic or suicidal. Contented is a much better target than euphoric. Happiness and depression are both exhausting. Contentment is sustainable. So when your wife has too much energy, go full flaps to slow her down. When she's in the doldrums, fire up that auxiliary engine to get back to cruising speed.

If the day ever comes when you're both in sync, you can put your marriage on autopilot and start living the dream.

PROTECTING THE EMPTY NEST

There used to be an ad on TV where the parents would tearfully send their adult child off into the world and then immediately convert his bedroom into a home theatre with a wet bar and a hot tub. The inference being that if his bedroom was gone, so was he. That's false advertising.

As a man, you have a clear understanding of the many phases of life. Being single, being married, having kids, raising kids, watching the kids move out, having your life back. Your wife, on the other hand, is a mother first and foremost and forever. Maybe it's because she's the one who gave birth or maybe it's just a woman's nature to be more giving. Maybe she just likes the kid better than you do. The reason is not nearly as important as the reality.

So if you're serious about not wanting your son to move back in after a few years of lacklustre results in the real world, you must have a plan. Don't bother turning his bedroom into a pleasuredome. Don't even bother moving into a one-bedroom condo. If he wants to move back in and your wife wants him there, it will happen. It may be a pull-out couch in the dining room with his clothes stuffed into the china cabinet, but it will happen.

It will happen because of two developments. The first will be him asking if he can move back home. The second will be your wife saying yes. You need a plan that will prevent at least one of those events from occurring.

Forget the second one. You are not capable of preventing that one from happening. Your wife is never going to turn her back on a whiny son in a million years. Even if she agrees to support your position of tough love by making the boy fend for himself, it will be a short-lived and miserable solution. She'll be upset and worried all the time and, worst of all, she'll blame *you*.

So forget the second event and focus on the first, which is your son asking if he can move back home. If you do it right, you can prevent that from happening. But you've got to start early. By the time he's three, you can start programming him to accept the importance of moving through all the stages of nature. Tell him about how the mother and father bird build a nest and hatch eggs and then feed the baby birds until they're old enough to fly. And once they fly away, they don't live in the nest anymore. Explain to him that if he ever does return to your nest, you will be sitting on him until he flies away for good.

As he gets older and starts to idolize Superman or Batman, point out to him how neither of those guys lives with their parents. Then, when he starts bringing girls over, behave badly. Underdress and play CDs of military music.

Let him know that you care about him and are there to help and support him, but don't ever allow him to think that living with his parents is his best or only option. If he doesn't *want* to move back home, that's half the battle. The other half is making sure he doesn't *need* to move back home. That will require an income. That will require him having a job. That's where you need to go to the fathers of his friends, because they're all in the same boat.

Nobody wants to ask their employer to hire their son, but they have no problem recommending a *friend's* son. So that's what you guys do. You form a brotherhood to make sure you keep each other's kids employed and solvent and out there in the big, big world where they can prosper rather than coming back into your tiny, tiny world and ruining everything.

MUCH ADO ABOUT TO DO

I remember years ago meeting an old guy who told me he had to get home and take care of his honeydews. I thought maybe that meant he was a melon farmer, which is how he struck me, but no, what he meant was "honey do's"—things his wife would tell him she needed to have done. Honey, do this; Honey, do that; Honey, stop touching me—that kind of thing. I'm sure it was all written down on a piece of paper.

I don't know if married couples do that anymore, where the wife will write up a "to do" list for the husband. Maybe she thinks it will annoy him to see her demands written out like that, especially if he's already busy with other things. Maybe she feels guilty in this age of equality—she doesn't want to look incapable of doing the things herself. Maybe the husband actually is annoyed at being handed a "to do" list on a Saturday morning when he was going to watch cartoons for a few hours and then just waste the rest of the day.

Well, if that's the case, then you guys need to give yourselves a shake. The "to do" list from your wife is one of the greatest boons to married life that you will ever experience. She's taken the time to write the jobs down clearly and legibly. That required her to think about all of them clearly and legibly. And she put them in a certain order based on importance or urgency or whatever.

The reason for the order is not important; the *order* is the key. If you're lucky enough to have a wife who would take the time to create a "to do" list, you need to treat her well. Don't whine or groan when she hands you the list. Give her a big smile and a kiss and thank her. Take the list, look it over, ask any questions to help clarify the items, fold it up neatly and put it into your shirt pocket.

And ask her for the pen. It's important that you get the pen.

Let me explain why these lists are such a boon for a husband. For starters, they may represent the only times in your entire married life when you will know what your wife wants. And you will know the order in which she wants it.

Also, the list, until you're handed the next one, is finite. So rather than facing an unending barrage of confusing complaints and suggestions, you have an itemized list—clear and legible—of what you can do to make her life better. In fact, I would suggest you go one step further and, before starting in on the list, you say to your wife, "I'm going to do everything on this list as quickly as I can and to the best of my ability, and I'm going to do them in the order you've asked because I want to do everything I can to give you a happy life. To help me do that, would you please put a number beside each job, showing how much happier you'll be, as a percentage of your current level of happiness, so I'll know for sure that what I'm doing is making you happy." Hand her the pen so she can write the percentages, but make sure you take it back. Then get to work. And as each job gets done, come and report to your wife and stand there until you can visibly see that she's exactly the percentage happier that she committed to.

The only wrinkle you'll encounter is that while you're doing one of the jobs and are nowhere near the end of the list, your wife will think of something else she'd like you to do. Again, rather than have a negative reaction, smile and thank her, but then hand her the list, and the pen, which you've guarded, and have her add the new item to the list in the spot where she thinks it should go. And remind her to include the percentage increase in her happiness once it's done.

Your marriage will be so happy, you won't know what to do with yourself. But that's okay, your wife will think of something to do with you.

THE REALITY GAME

A lot of women these days are watching those reality shows. The ones where people get voted off the island or are doing dumb things for money or are just living large and sleazy and letting the cameras capture it all. Often, their husbands are critical of these viewing choices and thereby make their marriages as volatile as the ones where the couples are getting paid to have arguments.

So if your wife is one of these women who really enjoy reality shows, I suggest you use that as an opportunity to get her to agree with you, rather than an opportunity for you to disagree with her.

To begin with, you need to watch the shows with her and pretend to enjoy them. Talk about the various strategies among the players and speculate as to how the contest is going to go. Even be the one who reminds her when the shows are on, so she doesn't miss them.

After a couple of months, start to make subtle comments that question the reality of reality shows. Like, if these people are deep in the Amazon rainforest, how do they find theatrical lighting? And when we see the contestants living in small huts made from wapiti dung and eating slugs and small lizards because that's the only food source, what about the crew? And the director? Is it possible that they're staying down the street at the Hyatt and eating at the Cracker Barrel? I would think so. They're not getting a big prize at the end. What cameraman in his right mind would give up working on *Jeopardy!* to go to Fiji and eat a monkey?

So now you've created doubt. Doubt about how real this reality is. Be upset about it. Tell her how disappointed you are to realize that you've been manipulated by these Hollywood producers. You got sucked in by the compelling premise that these were real people put in dangerous situations with real consequences. Sure, the scenery is nice and the people are somewhat attractive and a little interesting, but the main reason you were watching was the appeal of catching them off guard. Catching them being themselves.

To now suspect that the show is contrived, well, that's a setback and you're going to need a moment. This is like hiding in the bushes outside a neighbour's house and, when you peek in the window, you see them performing *Macbeth*. That's not satisfying.

Watch your wife's reaction. It may take a few weeks, but if you do it right, she may start to agree with you. Suddenly, she will start to lose interest in reality shows. This is when you have to make your move. You lament the downfall of reality shows because they were the only thing on television that wasn't scripted or contrived or somehow manipulated by producers and directors. She will agree. You will go on: Wouldn't it be great if there were true reality shows on television, with real people facing difficult challenges and with meaningful consequences? She will agree. You will go on further. (This may require fake surprise, as discussed in another part of this book.) Hey, wait a minute! There are shows like that on television! Lots of them! They're called *sports!*

Give it a try. It didn't work for me.

ACCOUNTING ERRORS

If you're the one who pays the bills in the family and you're feeling the crunch and you just can't take it anymore, you will be tempted to criticize your wife for the things she buys. It may be thirty or forty pairs of shoes that look identical to you, it may be weekly beauty treatments that, as far you're concerned, aren't working, it may be classes that she's taking to learn how to make useless, ugly things that she can display all over the house. Whatever it is, you have identified it as a waste of money and you want to confront her about it.

No, you don't. You are under the influence of Satan. He thrives on unhappy marriages and that's what you will have the moment you bring up this subject. You see the problem as the money she is spending. Even though you think that's what you're saying, that's not really what you're saying. Your message to her at that moment is this: "We used to have a certain level of scrutiny on purchases in this relationship and that has led us to a point where we are no longer financially viable, and therefore I am suggesting that we invoke a higher level of clearance for all of our purchases."

I know you didn't say that. I know you didn't say anything remotely like that. What you said was something like "You gotta back off on the Pilates. You're killing me here." But what she heard is the sentence I already told you. And since you live in a relationship of total equality, if the level of scrutiny has gone up for her purchases, it's also gone up for yours.

That's going to be a problem. Suddenly, your purchases will come under the same microscope. The boat, the Jet Ski, the snow-mobile, the ATV that you absolutely had to have that doesn't even run, the golf membership, the Cigar of the Month Club, the Red Green merchandise . . . the list goes on and on.

And it only gets worse. Not only will she compare the *number* of questionable expenditures, she'll also want to see the compa-rable *total costs* of those expenditures. That will not help you. She can get a whole lot of pedicures for the cost of a snowmobile. And she doesn't have to license or insure a pedicure.

So my advice is to do that math in your head long before you open your mouth. If the total cost of *your* ridiculous expenditures is greater than the total cost of *her* ridiculous expenditures, instead of calling her on them, you need to stay quiet and hope she does the same.

ONE THING AT A TIME

A common pattern we've all seen over the last few years is that someone will try some new behaviour, give it a fancy name and then present it as something we all should be doing. Before you know it, the activity reaches critical mass and each one of us starts to feel the pressure to change and start doing whatever this new thing is.

It happened with jogging and spinning and Zumba and Pilates and Texas hold 'em and unprotected sex. It seems like once these things gain some momentum, it's too late for the individual to evaluate and decline. Instead, you either have to participate or risk being left behind.

Well, under certain circumstances I'm saying it's better to be left behind. The one that comes to mind in particular is what they call multitasking. This is not a good or a natural way for a man to act. Women are much more suited to multitasking. God made them in such a way that they are able to produce offspring while holding down full-time employment. That's natural for them. So adding a few more simultaneous jobs to any workday is like falling off a log when you're a woman.

But since men have historically fallen off a lot more logs than women have, I'm here to tell you it's a stretch to make a man into a multitasker, and one of the best things you can do for your marriage is to convince your wife that multitasking is not your thing.

You don't want to take a bunch of jobs and do them all half-assed. You want to take one job and do it fully assed. That's what men do. When David slew Goliath, he didn't also have a load of laundry in. When Noah built the ark, he wasn't also managing a convenience store. The great accomplishments in history have not come from multitasking. They've come from *uni*-tasking— one thing at a time.

You need to explain to your wife that your mind and skill set are not as sophisticated as hers. And they never will be, if you have anything to say about it. You are a born uni-tasker and proud of it. You will do anything for her as long as you can do it as a free-standing project. You like songs, not medleys; you like roses, not bouquets; your favourite colour is blue, not plaid. Being a uni-tasker allows you to focus on one job at a time and, more important, it forces your wife to focus on just one of your jobs at a time. That way, if you're going off track, it's only in one area, not in the entire range of marital activity.

You were born a uni-tasker and that's the way you and God want to keep it. Point out to her that whenever a man is forced to be a multitasker, he ends up living in a compound with seven wives.

WE ARE NOT WORTHY

When I was a kid, I used to watch the *Wild Kingdom* TV show with Marlin Perkins, an old guy who would go out into the wilderness of Africa in a veiled attempt to kill his assistant, Jim.

The spring episodes were the best, the ones showing the males of the herd fighting for supremacy. There could only be one top dog, or in this case, antelope or ram or lion or elephant or rhinoceros or elk. It would start with one male honking his horn or bellowing his bellows or stomping on the ground or sending some other signal that he was in charge and that he would be the alpha male for the entire herd, deciding where they would go and where they would live and who would do what and that, most important, he would have his pick of all the females. Some of the other males would just accept that as a no-brainer. This guy was bigger and stronger than them and they didn't have any issues with accepting authority.

But there would always be a couple of males who questioned this guy's right to be in charge. If we're talking about rams, for example, whichever of them felt like it could challenge the guy to a head-butting contest. So they'd run at each other headfirst a couple of times. Pretty soon, the one with the softer head would reconsider. Suddenly, making the headache stop seemed a more pressing objective than being king of the herd. Maybe he'd start to think that even the best-looking female sheep aren't all that attractive.

But the interesting part of the process to me, was that the next day everything was fine. The lead guy didn't kill anybody and the one who lost totally accepted the supremacy of the winner. Life goes on and the herd flourishes in peace.

I don't think human beings are a lot different than that. Men don't fight over who gets his pick of the women, because we've evolved to the point where women make their own choices. But men still need to know who's in charge, and they need to feel that whoever is in charge is doing not necessarily a good job, but certainly a better job than they would do.

People may think that men need to be the boss, but that's not true. If they're the one best suited to be the boss, then sure, that's what they should be, but if they know the current boss is doing at least as good a job as they would, they're fine with being in a subordinate role.

The two unhappiest men in the world are the one who isn't the boss and should be, and the one who shouldn't be the boss, but is. And when it comes to marriage, my opinion is that the man should never be the boss. Be an adviser to the boss, be a consultant to the boss, always be at the ready with prompt and courteous service.

I know this is a tough message for all you alpha males out there. I know you want to be the one making the decisions, but if the only decisions that stick are the ones your wife approves of, that means they really aren't your decisions in the first place.

So just accept the subordinate position, as if the big showdown was yesterday and now it's time for your personal herd to flourish in peace. Otherwise, you're going to have a lifetime of head-butting.

THE QUICKEST WAY

We've all heard that the quickest way to a man's heart is through his stomach. I'm not sure everyone believes that, and I especially hope the cardio surgeons don't. But there is probably some logic behind the theory that, since men enjoy eating in a basic, visceral way—not as a social endeavour, but as a plain and simple physical pleasure—that fact creates a vulnerability that women don't have. Which means that men could be capable of taking their positive feeling from eating and equating that to love.

Men are certainly capable of going the other way—taking a feeling of love and equating it to physical pleasure by the third date at the latest. Maybe some of you out there are married to a woman who is a great cook, and maybe it's one of the reasons you were attracted to her in the first place and continue to live your life with her despite some other incompatibilities in the marriage. After all, the average couple only has sex once a week, but almost everybody eats three times a day.

But at this moment I'm not talking to any guy whose wife is a great cook. I'm talking to the other guys—the ones whose wives regularly make meals that are barely edible. I know you're disappointed, I know you feel cheated. Maybe this is all coming as a shock to you. Perhaps you should have focused less on premarital sex and more on premarital home-cooked meals.

I also know that you are strongly tempted to criticize your wife for being incompetent in that area. You may even want to point out what a great cook your mother was, if you have the guts. But this is not a question of guts; this is about stupidity. It is absolutely idiotic for you to criticize your wife's cooking. Instead, here's the path I suggest.

After you've been married long enough to realize your wife has some serious deficiencies when it comes to preparing meals, start to secretly save samples of various meals in a thermos or hermetically sealed container of some kind. I don't actually know what a hermetically sealed container is, but I really enjoyed saying it.

After a week or so of collecting these samples, take them to a chemist or a doctor or a toxicologist, anybody who can determine the health risks of consuming these foods. Chances are the results will show that your wife is not trying to kill you. That's always good news, and in this case it's all you need to know. My advice is to immediately stop yourself from complaining about anything she cooks. Even if you have to stop breathing so you don't taste it, or consciously quell your gag reflex, it's in your best interest not to be negative.

Instead, dwell on the positive. If she ever does cook anything that's half-decent, make a big deal out of it so she'll do it again. Your reaction to her cooking should be either positive or non-existent. No negative stuff. Mainly you should express gratitude, and I'll tell you why: the difference in cost between you eating at home and eating at a restaurant is, conservatively, $50 per day, which translates to $18,250 a year, which, over a fifty-year marriage, totals almost a million dollars. No matter how bad your wife's cooking is, it's going to make you a millionaire. And you'll never get fat from overeating. I don't see a downside.

HANDSOME HANDY

Despite your best efforts to make her happy, after a while your wife may seem to lose some of her enthusiasm for the marriage and, if she can sustain her dark mood for long enough, there's a chance you will eventually notice.

There are a lot of potential reasons why your relationship has lost some of its lustre since the wedding, but in most cases she's unhappy because she doesn't have enough closet space. This is an excellent opportunity for you to demonstrate that you are the perfect husband as you show off your handyman skills to solve the problem quickly and cost-effectively.

Here's an ideal project for those of you who live in rural areas, where there are no inspectors or building codes. You city dwellers are out of luck, but that's what you get for trying to show off.

The first thing you need is a 1985 or older Dodge Magic Wagon. These babies have fallen on hard times since the introduction of emissions testing, and nobody knows how to get rid of them. They have no resale value, they're too big to bury and it's hard to burn one without drawing attention. You should try to get a dark green model so that the combination of the forest hue with the rusty edges makes the van blend right in with your shrubbery.

Now, pick an outside wall of your bedroom. You're going to knock a hole in that wall to provide access to your minivan closet. If the minivan runs, you can actually use it to knock out the hole, and as a bonus, it will be the perfect size.

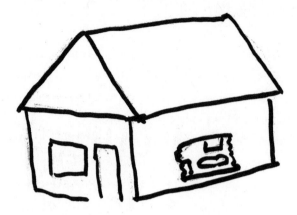

Next, get a large child's inflatable wading pool—no, wait, make that a child's large inflatable wading pool. Blow it up and mount it over the hole, with the floor of the pool up against the outside wall of the house.

Cut out the floor of the pool and save it to use as a waterproof bedsheet in case you ever have kids or get old. Next, parallel-park the van in such a way that the sliding side door forms a weatherproof seal with the inflated pool rings.

Take all the seats out of the van and use them to redo your family room. (Make sure you and your wife get the front seats. They're recliners.) Get yourself a dozen or more toilet plungers. (Try gas station restrooms.) Smear the edges of the plungers with Vaseline. (If you've ever been to a frat party, you've done this before.) Now install the plungers on the inside of the van windows, using their own suction. Stagger them to maximize the storage capacity. Remove the convex mirror from the passenger door and mount it on the inside wall of the van. The wide-angle image will allow your wife to model her entire outfit and is also very slimming. It's a win-win.

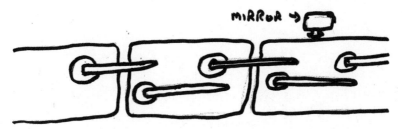

Place a couple of small stepladders side by side in the cargo area. Use empty pizza boxes (small to extra-large) as shelves to hold her shoes—that's logical; they're *step*ladders. (Let's all take a moment to enjoy that one.)

Dedicate the centre console to holding her frilly undergarments. As an added touch of elegance, throw in a car air freshener. There's nothing sexier than a woman in silk lingerie with just a hint of pine scent. Clip her brooches and hair accessories onto the steering wheel and slide her rings and bracelets onto the turn-signal lever.

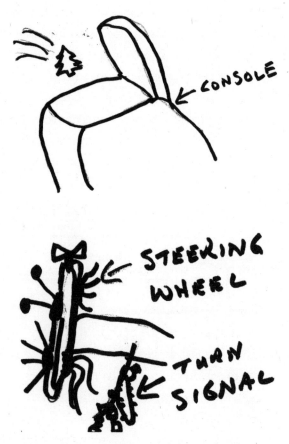

Now just put her clothes in there and get ready for the look on her face! If the van runs, she can have the closet heated and air-conditioned. Even if it doesn't, leave the battery hooked up so the light will go on when she opens the door and she can listen to AM or FM radio or her favourite 8-tracks. You can even give her the key so she can lock you out. And I'm pretty sure she will.

CARING IS THE HARDEST PART

Anybody who works as a negotiator or a mediator or a marriage counsellor or a broadloom salesman knows that the most important factor when offering service is to find the common ground between the two parties. Or between the customer and a braided twill Oriental rug that's been sitting in your showroom for seven years. And the first step in finding that common ground is to identify what is important to each person.

One of the biggest challenges facing men and women who are trying to cohabitate is the startling differences in what they care about. And it applies to all areas of their lives. I'm not going to include every one of them here because it will take up too much time and space and it may prevent me from getting to write another book. So here are just enough to prove my point.

1) What we care about on a date.
    Women: Looking my best.
            Being treated with respect.
            Being able to tell my friends how great the date was.
            Being able to tell my dad that he was wrong about Herb.
    Men: Surviving the date.
            Avoiding criticism.
            Getting as far into the date as possible before the

hope of any kind of intimacy becomes completely out of the question.

2) What we care about when we're driving.
   Women: Driving safely.
           Being courteous and law-abiding.
           Looking good.
           Arriving at the destination at some point.
   Men: Nobody passes me.
           Nobody tailgates me.
           Nobody holds me up.
           Looking tough.
           Arriving at the destination at least ten minutes faster than the last time I went there.

3) What we care about when we're dining.
   Women: Looking refined and elegant.
           Undereating.
           Making intelligent conversation.
   Men: Demonstrating appetite as a measure of manliness.
           I shouldn't have to pay and eat vegetables.
           If I buy dinner, I will have expectations.
           If I buy an expensive dinner, I will have great expectations.

4) What we care about when we're watching a movie.
   Women: Something that touches my heart and my mind.
           A well-written, compelling story, performed by great actors.
   Men: Action. Or huge belly laughs. Or the ultimate: action that causes huge belly laughs.
           Popcorn.
           Necking.

5) What we care about when going shopping.
   Women: This is a sightseeing adventure where I'll have fun discovering all of the retail items that are currently available at all price levels and in all colours.
   I don't care how long it takes.

   Men: This is a mission. I'm going to go in there, buy the specific item I went for and get the hell out.
   I'll give it ten minutes plus travel time.

6) What we care about when making a purchase.
   Women: Value.
   Brand name.
   Sophistication.

   Men: The lowest price.
   The salesman needs to know that I am richer than him.
   My buddies are gonna be so jealous when I tell them I bought this.

7) What we care about when our kids play sports.
   Women: My child needs to treat the other team with respect and kindness.
   My child will learn the importance of getting along with others.

   Men: My child needs to win the game.
   My child needs to win the fights.
   I will show my child how to berate the referee/umpire/other coach/other team/parents of the other team.

8) What we care about when our spouse is upset.
   Women: Identifying the cause of the upset.
   What can I do to help?
   I love you no matter what.

Men:	How long is this gonna go on?
	It's not my problem, what can I do?
	This is not my fault no matter what.

A CLOSED SYSTEM

I thought this might be a good moment to remind you of why you're making all this effort and all these compromises and radical changes to your life just to keep your wife happy, and to encourage you to keep doing it for as long as humanly possible.

Let's start by observing a man who is the exact opposite of a fully functioning husband. This is a man who has no interaction with anyone—not physical, not spiritual, not confrontational, not even conversational. This is a guy who has no family and no friends. A complete and total loner. There isn't one person in the world he can share ideas or stories with, which would be fine except that humans are social animals and have a basic need to share ideas and stories. Because of that, this guy begins to share ideas and stories with himself.

And it goes really well. No arguments, no disagreements, no eye-rolling. Just the satisfying feeling of laying out this litany of amazing theories with absolutely no opposition.

After doing this for a while, this man starts to believe he must be the smartest person who ever lived. Everything he says is accepted by his audience (him) as yet another inspired revelation. Pretty soon he feels that he needs to share this brilliance with the world, not for the purpose of having them benefit from his insights, but for the purpose of having them stand in awe and then bow down.

So he starts standing on street corners and advising passing strangers about how he would balance the budget and how to get all the toothpaste out of the tube. It's only a matter of time until he's living under a bridge in a cardboard box and talking to squirrels.

You don't want to be that guy. When you don't have someone to interact with, you're in a closed system. On a spreadsheet, it's called a circular reference. It's not valid because there is not enough outside information—the formula is just spinning its wheels. You don't want to be spinning your wheels. You need outside input in your life. Food, water, air and alcohol are not enough. You need at least one person to talk to, or you're going to have a completely skewed self-image—perhaps an inferiority complex, but probably not.

And to be the most effective partner, that other person needs to have two things: freedom and dependence. I know those things sound like opposites, and they are, unless that person is your significant other. They're the only ones who have the freedom to tell you their opinion, point-blank, right between the eyes (which is what you need), and yet have the dependence of having committed to spend their lives with you and therefore have a vested interest in your future.

No friend will give you that. Squirrels won't give you that. You can give it to yourself, but that doesn't count.

So take a deep breath and get back to the task at hand, which is finding ways to get along better with your wife. She's the one who'll give you a home. Throw the cardboard box into the recycling bin.

EQUAL BUT NOT INTERCHANGEABLE

There has been a constant pressure to make men and women equal, and by now we all agree that it's the only fair and just way to be. Some think it started in the '60s, or maybe when the women got the vote, but I think it started around the beginning of time.

You can't have two partners in a relationship, mutually dependent, without having that equality reflected in all parts of society. But I think where we go too far is when we equate equality with interchangeability. That's wrong. There are situations where one sex is clearly preferred over the other. The restroom attendant at a gentleman's club needs to be a man. The mammogram technician needs to be a woman.

But the proof of my argument lies in the phrases and sentences that people use on a regular basis. When you try to make them apply equally to both sexes, as I have below, you will see that it just doesn't work:

- (He/She) has great legs.
- I think (he/she) is wearing too much eye shadow.
- I find it unattractive when I can see (his/her) bra straps.
- (He/She) was sweating like a pig.
- (He/She) has an incredible amount of back hair.
- (He/She) was relieving (himself/herself) against a tree.
- (He/She) has a receding hairline and a full beard.
- That skirt is way too tight on (him/her).
- That (waiter/waitress) is showing way too much cleavage.
- (He/She) can bench press four hundred pounds.
- That outfit looks a little effeminate on (him/her).
- (He/She) was sitting on the back porch having a beer and enjoying a big fat stogey when, for no reason, (he/she) leaned over in (his/her) chair and broke wind.
- (He/She) is a perfect 38-24-36.
- (He/She) delivered a nine-pound baby.
- As a result, (he/she) is having a vasectomy.

TO KNOW HER IS TO LOVE HER

The biggest enemy to a successful marriage in the long term is not anger or even mild dislike. It's apathy. You get to the point where you don't even care enough to try to make things better. You just get quiet and live your own life inside of your married life. This is not good. And one day, probably right after your doctor's appointment, you will suddenly realize that this is your life and it sucks and you'll do something radical that will be bad for you and your family and all of the other customers at Hooters.

Don't let it get that far. Work at keeping your relationship alive and vibrant. The first step in doing that is to check your current status *vis à vis* how much time and energy you are putting into making your wife happy. The first step in doing *that* is for you to realize that you may no longer know your wife nearly as well as you used to.

Here's a little quiz that will help you identify how little you know about your wife. You have to do the test by yourself. You can't look at your wife or her picture or ask her masseuse. You're on your own.

1) What colour are your wife's eyes?
2) What colour is your wife's favourite dress?
3) What colour is your wife's hair?
4) What colour is your wife?
5) What is her favourite song? (Hint: Probably not an anthem.)
6) Could you pick your wife out of a crowd?
7) If so, how big a crowd? (Three people, no matter how big they are, is not a crowd.)
8) Do you *really* know what she looks like, or would you just be hoping to recognize her coat?
9) If she were kidnapped, would your description of her cause the police to stop looking and arrest you for homicide?
10) How many times have the two of you gone out together in the last five years, not counting house fires?

11) Would you take a bullet for her?

12) Would you take a phone message for her?

13) Does your wife often say a short phrase to you that ends with the word *off*?

14) Would your wife marry you again if you asked her?

15) Would you ask her?

16) What is your favourite thing about your wife? (Ten-minute time limit.)

17) If marriage is a competition, in your opinion, which of you won? (A tie doesn't necessarily mean there's no loser. It could be quite the opposite.)

LEAVE ME ALONE

Once you're twenty years or more into this thing, your wife will probably start focusing on your personal health. She'll start reading articles about what happens to men's bodies after years of neglect. She may encourage you to join a fitness club, and by "encourage" I mean order.

She'll present you with meals that are made entirely of organic vegetables. She'll pull you away from the buffet table by clenching your love handles. She'll shred all your cigarettes and sell your ashtrays on eBay. And you know what she's really up to. She's not just trying to insult you or abuse you; she's trying to save you from yourself. She wants your life to be as long and healthy as possible. And you know that's a huge compliment because it means she enjoys having you around and would miss you terribly if you weren't there.

And yet you still find it incredibly annoying. You'll come up with plenty of reasons why you shouldn't bother changing to a healthier lifestyle. You'll mention George Burns smoking cigars at a hundred or Colonel Sanders, who was lickin' his fingers well into his eighties. You may even point out random old fat people to support your case, but be careful, because fat people are usually a lot younger than they look.

You can play the fate card—saying your genetics, not your lifestyle, are the key factor in longevity. But then she'll mention that you don't have a male relative who lived past the age of fifty, and most of them died holding a large draft and a handful of cheese curds. Her argument is that you inherit more from your fridge than from your family.

So let's get real here. All of your excuses are just a smokescreen. The truth is, you don't want to change. You're happy being overweight and out of shape. You don't need to be in shape; you're not a professional athlete. And you don't need to look good; you're married. You're not going to make the kinds of changes she wants because you're not motivated.

The reason you're not motivated is because you don't think you're going to have a heart attack. Not right now, anyway. Maybe ten years from now you should revisit the subject. But for now, why fix something that feels good? The problem here is with the actual nature of heart attacks. If they were more like facial hair, life would be so much simpler. With facial hair, you start with none, and then you gradually notice soft blond hairs growing on your chin, and then, eventually, there are enough of them that you do a little trimming, and then they start growing in thick and black, and at that point, you start shaving. The whole process can take a year or two. Heart attacks are instantaneous.

I'm sure lots of out-of-shape, overweight men have said, "I never had a heart problem in my life, and now here I am, dead." Or they *would* have said that. So until you are convinced that you are absolutely on the path to a heart attack, you're not going to make any serious changes. That will prompt your wife to get you more information. And her way of doing that is to book you a doctor's appointment.

Women often ask me why men hate to go to the doctor. I'll tell you why: men don't like reality; we like fantasy. We use our imaginations to make our lives better. That's how we survive ho-hum jobs or ho-hum marriages or ho-hum lives. Women like reality. Men avoid it. And there's no worse reality than a doctor's examination. It's like a mechanic looking at your car. If he doesn't find something wrong, he's out of business.

There is no upside when a man goes to the doctor. The best he can hope for is that the doctor will tell him he's as healthy as he thought he was. That's called the status quo. That's not good news. That's how he felt going in there. So really, from a man's perspective, the only reason to see a doctor is to get bad news.

I'm not saying that's right, I'm just saying that's true.

Of course, a rational person would argue that for many diseases, early detection is key and you won't get that without a doctor's exam. But men are warped and many of them would prefer to think they're healthy longer than to know they're sick sooner. That's why we need to marry women who are prepared to keep annoying us to the point where the path of least resistance* becomes a healthier lifestyle and regular checkups.

YOU TELL ME

From Buster's diary:

Dear Diary,

I thought after eighteen years of marriage I would have figured this out. I know I'm not completely stupid—I've been able to hold down a seasonal job year after year, and I tie my own shoelaces on a regular basis. I'm pretty good with computers and there's not an internal combustion engine on the planet

---

* See "Path of Least Resistance," somewhere else in this book.

that I can't rebuild. So why, after all this time, does my wife continue to not make any sense to me? Yesterday was her birthday, as you know from my entries every other year around this time. And as you'll recall, it has never been a good day for me. I don't ever seem to get it right—one year I bought her socket wrenches, another time I was on a business trip and didn't call (they don't allow cellphones in strip clubs), one year I enrolled her in Weight Watchers—nothing pleases her. So this year I took a whole different approach. I thought it would be fun to play a little trick on her by just pretending I'd forgotten it was her birthday. It wasn't hard. I just remembered the year I really did forget her birthday and then just acted like that. It was pretty funny, but she didn't actually get the joke at first. Or ever. Instead of giggling about it like a normal person would do, she got real chippy. She ate her breakfast in the bathroom and made me pour my own coffee. I was concerned that she was okay, so I yelled, "What's your problem?" through the bathroom door. I'm gonna leave her response out of this diary because my grandchildren may be reading this one day. I asked her to open the door so we can discuss this like adults. She opened the door and then hit me in the face with a wet towel, so at least we were communicating again. She started yelling at me with a barrage of uncomplimentary names. You'd think she'd loaded a thesaurus of obscene insults into an AK-47 and then aimed it at me and squeezed the trigger until all the ammo was gone. I remember thinking to myself, "This is not going well." She didn't believe me when I told her I hadn't forgotten her birthday and that this was all a joke. She said something like, "It's not a joke! Jokes are funny!" So I showed her the proof. I reached into my back pocket and pulled out a birthday card that I presented to her, with a big smile. "See? It was a joke." And I laughed. All by myself. In hindsight, the whole joke thing may have been an error in judgment. And maybe I should have gotten her a gift or flowers or something. And it was probably wrong to say, "I figured you didn't want to be reminded of how old you are." But I did get her a really nice, romantic card, which she would have noticed if she'd read it. Or opened it. Or not thrown it into the woodstove. Instead, she put on her ski jacket and headed off to Walmart to get herself "something special." And her parting shot as she went out the door was to tell me that getting her a card, rather than an actual gift, was way worse than me forgetting it was her birthday. So there is some good news—next year I won't bother with the card.

THE FOUNTAIN OF YOUTH

As time goes by in your marriage, you may start to notice that your wife's appearance is changing. I'm not talking about weight gain or hairstyles. I mean a few lines and wrinkles here and there, some sagging, some dragging, some full-out saddle-bagging. You might even be tempted to point out these changes. That would be very foolish. Instead, get out your wedding pictures and prop them up beside the bathroom mirror so you can compare how *you* look now with how you looked then. You will come to one of three conclusions:

1) You are aging faster than your wife. This is the one to strive for. It will make your wife happy to be mistaken for your daughter. It will make you proud to be with such a vibrant young woman. And it will make strangers think you must be a millionaire or a Don Juan—or a millionaire Don Juan—to have such a young wife.

2) You and your wife are aging at the same rate. This is fine. It leads to compatibility and companionship. In the

race to the grave, you and your wife are running neck and neck. Not a bad way to go.

3) **Your wife is aging faster than you are.** This one is trouble. She's not going to take it as a compliment when strangers think she's your mother. You have to do something about this situation. You might be able to get by for a while by hiring a makeup artist and lighting director for her. You could even look into cosmetic surgery. If she's not willing to have procedures done that will make her look younger, you'll need to have some done that will make you look older. That'll work for a few years.

However, if you're looking for a permanent solution, that'll be trickier. There are several factors that affect the rate of aging in a person. Certainly, diet, exercise and genetics are important, but the crucial component is the treatment a person gets from their partner. A person who does not feel appreciated, respected or loved will age faster. You're okay because you provide all of those things to yourself. But how do you treat your wife? A self-centred, demanding person can actually suck the life out of their partner.

If your wife is aging faster than you are, you could be the cause of that. Start by doing something that makes her happy. No, wait. Start with finding out what makes her happy and then do that. Even Methuselah looks younger when he's smiling. Especially when he cleans his tooth. Mainly, you have to adjust your attitude. You're both in this for the long haul and it's way healthier to make the best of the life changes you're gonna face, not to mention the face changes life's gonna make.

INVASION OF THE BODY SNATCHERS

I know there are skeptics out there who don't believe anything, and I'm not an easy person to convince, either, but I think when you're faced with overwhelming evidence, you have to accept the only logical explanation. At least until something better comes along.

Pay close attention—this could happen to you. Let's say you're married to a woman who is over the age of forty and you start to notice radical behavioural changes. She's irritable; she's weepy; she sleeps a lot; she has strange cravings; when she's with people, she wants to be alone; when she's alone, she doesn't want to be left alone.

Now, doctors and psychologists will tell you this is something called "menopause." Don't believe it. There is no way the woman that you fell in love with and married could change this suddenly or severely. *Menopause* is a Greek word for "cover-up." What's actually happened is that your wife's body has been taken over by aliens. They are from another planet and know nothing about earth or married life or you. They can't even figure out our climate as they try to manage your wife's heating and cooling systems.

And the cute little things that you do that your wife used to find amusing, they find annoying. They find loud noises are much too loud and silence is way too quiet. They sometimes look at you like they don't know you and they look like if they did know you, they would kill you. This can't possibly be your wife. Oh sure, she's still in there somewhere, but these aliens are clearly in control. Why else would she be refusing to do housework? Refusing to be civil? Refusing to be herself?

Only aliens would ask you questions like "Did you know life would be this miserable when you married me? Come on, yes or no?" Only aliens would watch *Mary Poppins* and start sobbing uncontrollably. It wasn't *that* bad.

And when you wake up in the middle of the night and see there's a light on in the kitchen and you go down there to find your wife eating ice cream out of the container with a fork and she yells at you to go back to bed, that's not her—that's a creature from Mars protecting a discovery. They don't have ice cream on Mars, let alone forks.

So just ignore what the medical community tells you about so-called menopause. This isn't hormone imbalance. It's *cosmic* imbalance. You just need to be supportive and keep your distance for the next ten years or so. Your wife is still in there. She'll take over again once the aliens leave. And they will eventually leave because being a married woman is too tough for any other species or genetic mutation from any other planet. Slowly but surely they'll abandon their mission, and as each one goes, your wife will become more and more like the person she was before it all began.

But don't ever tell your wife that for the last ten years she was possessed by aliens from outer space. Unless you want to see some flying saucers.

SEE YOU IN COURT

Throughout the course of any relationship you're going to have disagreements, and for the relationship to survive, you're going to need to learn how to resolve your differences and how to arrive at fair and equitable solutions that treat each party with respect and make them feel that things are going to get better.

Other than King Solomon, nobody has ever been born knowing how to do this. It's a learned skill. They teach the art of negotiating at several colleges, for those of you who have time to go to college, and there are weekend seminars if you're embarrassed about being older than the prof.

But for my money, the most effective way to learn how to deal with a domestic dispute is to sit in the gallery at a small claims court. You need to listen carefully to the cases as presented by the plaintiffs and defendants. You'll find yourself much better at reaching logical conclusions when you watch strangers argue than you are when you and your wife are having the disagreement. That's because there is no baggage when strangers fight and you have no emotional attachment. You can even make a bit of a game out of comparing your verdict to the one ultimately handed down by the judge.

But make no mistake, the main purpose of your visit is to study the judge and emulate his every action. Watch the way he focuses on each party as they present their case. Listen to the intelligent questions he asks. Observe as he expertly leads them to see the case in an objective light as he gives them a chance to discover who is at fault, what the damages are, and what would be a reasonable plan of restitution.

These are the skills you want to take home with you. The ability to stay calm and unemotional and to judge the case on its own merits alone. Not on something that you're still mad about that happened during the wedding reception involving your wife's brother and a gallon of corn oil.

You can learn a lot from a small claims court judge. How to be reasonable, how to be unbiased, how to uphold the letter of the law and, most important, how to fake being interested in anything that's being said. That's the real key.

YOU NEED A REFEREE

Verbal communication between a husband and a wife is a very complex issue. That's because there are six different versions of each and every statement. They can be divided in the categories of Theoretical and Factual, with three versions in each category.

In the Theoretical category, we have what you think you said, what you think you heard and what you think you think. On the

Factual side, we have what you actually said, what you really heard and what you truly think. And the confusing aspect of these six versions is that you are wishing and hoping, and therefore programmed to believe, that the theoretical versions are correct. In our minds, what we *think* we said always dominates what we *actually* said. Even when we know what we actually said, we will deny, deny, deny because we don't like it as much as what we think we said. And your partner is operating under exactly the same premise.

Try to imagine how many millions of arguments are started when what he thinks he said doesn't match what she thinks she heard. Is there any hope for a husband and wife to have successful verbal communication? No. Not without an objective frame of reference in the mix. When you and your wife are getting along great, you need to be alone. But when you're having a serious argument, you need someone else there. Some person or authority that both of you accept as the arbiter of the truth. This is how marriage counsellors came to be. The fact that we can't accept what we actually think or said or heard creates the need for someone who can.

Sometimes they work and sometimes they don't, but the simple concept of having an objective third party in on the conversation is really the main value they provide. When you've got a referee there, you're going to try to make yourself look better—i.e., not stupid. The referee won't care what you *think* you said or heard or think, they will only care about what you *truly* said or heard or think. And that will force you to do the same.

Or maybe you could just record every conversation you have with your wife and then play it back when there's a disagreement. But as soon as your wife realizes you recorded her, you're a dead man, even if you're right.

So I recommend you find yourself a referee. Not a friend of yours and not a friend of your wife's. Someone you both dislike equally. And don't set it up like you're blatantly looking for a ruling. Try to recreate the conversation that started the problem, but this time include the referee in the discussion and you will dramatically increase your chances of having a better outcome.

Nine times out of ten, when the referee gives their opinion, you're going to like what you hear. Or at least what you think you hear.

THE FUTURE OF EVOLUTION

Any anthropologist worth his sea salt will tell you that animals evolve based on their environment and behaviour. That's how fish got wings and dogs got teeth and McDonalds got over thirty thousand franchises. Similarly, the human body has the amazing ability to morph over time so that it is better suited to what it's being used for. This process is going to make relationships between men and women even more difficult as they evolve farther and farther apart. We all need to be aware of this issue so that we can change our behaviour and thereby minimize its effect. If we don't do anything, here's how I see men and women looking in another thousand years:

Women

Large, sympathetic eyes and huge, thick lips on expressionless faces as body adapts by producing its own collagen and Botox.

Knee-length arms to allow for shopping bags on wheels to be pulled without bending over.

Men

Compound eyes to allow for simultaneous viewing of multiple television channels. Very small ears due to habit of not listening. Extension of lower jaw to allow snacks to be top-loaded.

Large thumb with narrow tip and extra knuckle to allow for more efficient use of remote. Large, heavy butt so he can fall asleep at his desk without falling over.

Beware of evolution—it could happen to you!

MOVIN' ON

Everybody knows that about half of all marriages end in divorce. It's not a happy situation, but if this happens to you and there is no hope of reconciliation, the most important thing for each of you is to find a way to move on.

This is a major life change. It's a milestone, where you have to put the past behind you and focus instead on what's in front of you. Over the centuries, humans have built ceremonies around milestones like these—marriages, funerals, puberty, etc. It helps the people and their friends and relatives accept the new reality and find a way forward.

So instead of just getting a divorce, I suggest you give it a special ceremony. It's a big deal and it deserves a ceremony. It's like a marriage, only backwards. At a wedding, you go in single and come out married. This one is the exact opposite. So you need to do it backwards. Start with the reception and end with the ceremony. And everything about it should reinforce the divorce theme.

Don't have it in your apartment—call a real estate agent and see if he can lend you a fully detached new listing. Have the dinner menu imply "divorce"—I suggest oysters on the half shell and a banana split. Let the guests know that every time they clink their glasses, you and your wife will stand up and give each other the finger. Once the speeches and bad jokes are done, have a divorce lawyer come up and perform the ceremony.

Here again, I would suggest you model the presentation after the standard wedding vows. Just make a few minor changes:

The Divorce Vows

Lawyer: We are gathered here to unhitch these two hearts in the bonds of unholy divorce. If anyone present can show just and legal cause why they should stay married, let them pay my fee or forever hold their peace.
(To the Congregation) Who takes this woman from this man?
(A young, good-looking fitness trainer stands at the back of the room, smiles and winks at the lawyer. The lawyer winks back and turns to the couple.)
John, will you have this woman removed as your awful wedded partner, as a joint tenant and tax deduction, as you return to the swinging single life?

John: I will.

Lawyer: Will you avoid her, dishonour her and generally
            ignore her, no matter how sick she gets, and,
            forsaking all STD warnings, be unfaithful to her
            for as long as you both shall live?

John: I will.

Lawyer: Jane, will you take this man for everything you
            can, to live in his current home while he resides in
            his car?

Jane: I will.

Lawyer: Will you badmouth him, ridicule him, distribute
            embarrassing pictures of him and, forsaking all
            others, reiterate each and every one of his inad-
            equacies in the bedroom, for as long as you both
            shall live?

Jane: I will.

            *(John and Jane take off their wedding rings and
            hand them to the lawyer. He holds them up.)*
            Behold these symbols of wedlock. The perfect
            circle of love, the unbroken union of these two
            souls. They're toast.
            *(He tosses the rings off to the side. The maid
            of honour catches them in a garbage can and
            hands both of them to the bride, who puts them
            in her purse.)*
            Please lock eyes and repeat after me: I, John
            (Jane), reject thee, Jane (John), as my wedded
            partner, to halve and to hold, for richer (Jane) or
            poorer (John), in slickness or in stealth, to lust
            and to flourish, till death do its part. For as much
            as John, and especially Jane, have begrudgingly
            consented to this divorce, and have witnessed the
            same before what's left of their family and friends,
            and have given and pledge their vendettas to each

other, and have declared the same by removing their rings and sneering, by authority vested me by the State of Matrimony, I pronounce this couple to be separated in divorce. *(To John and Jane)* You may bicker.
(John and Jane launch into bitter argument. Congregation joins in. Lawyer mingles, handing out business cards.)

MYSTERY SOLVED

For many years, the medical community and insurance companies have been stumped by the superior health, stamina and longevity of women. If you study physiology at all, you'll find out that women have less muscle, less bone and more fat than men.

Now, I don't know what you've heard, but according to my doctor and my wife, who occasionally are the same person, fat is not a good thing. When was the last time any health-services person ever advised you to eat more cheeseburgers and fries rather than the yogurt and veggies you crave? Never.

They tell you to look for "fat-free," not "fat-laden." So how can the people who have more natural fat—i.e., women—be healthier than the muscular folks—i.e., us?

And they give birth! If I ever gave birth, I'd be lying down and whining about it forever. If it didn't kill me, I would regret that. Members of the weaker sex, who have less muscle, less bone and more fat, who give birth by creating another person inside their bodies and then expel that person through an orifice of a totally inappropriate size, not only survive, but actually outlive their partners, who have all the strength and none of the work.

How can that be? Nobody knows the answer, except me. But before I tell you, let me tease you a little bit. Have you ever been on a road trip with your wife and she has to go to the bathroom desperately and insists that you pull off the highway right now, even though you had planned to go another three hundred miles before stopping?

If the car is overheating or you're short on fuel or you have a soft tire, you'll pull over in a flash, but for something as manageable as a bathroom break, you have a problem. Your first thought is, "Why didn't she go at the restaurant where we had breakfast? Or the gas station where I filled up before we hit the freeway?" But you don't say any of those things because you've said them before and the answers were unsatisfying and negatively impacted your enjoyment of the holiday.

So instead, you sigh and say something under your breath and then pull over at the next exit. You then pull into a gas station, but rather than go to the pumps, you drive right up to the restrooms so that all of the other men will understand the situation and silently feel your pain. Then your wife will get out of the car, go inside to get the key because you refused to go into a strange gas station to ask for the key to the ladies' washroom, just in case the clerk misunderstood your intentions and was armed. And as you sit in the car, you see your wife go into the station and then come out with the key and then go into the restroom—two, three, four—then come out with the key and return it to the station and then come back to the car and tell you we need to go somewhere else because that restroom was "icky."

Or how about the time you booked a cabin for the weekend and the two of you went up there for a romantic getaway and everything was great until your wife found out there was an outhouse rather than indoor plumbing, and that was the end of your weekend.

Have you figured it out yet? No? Well, let's work backwards. The reason women hate outhouses and "icky" restrooms is because they sit down to go to the bathroom. Most of the time, we don't. So we don't care how disgusting the seat is, we won't be on it.

And we've all heard those stories about snakes or other animals coming up through the hole of an outhouse. Well, a man will see it coming, whereas a woman is blindsided. And that's why women have the superior life expectancy.

It's that simple. It's all because they always sit down to go to the bathroom.

Think about it: if you, as a manly man, go five or six times a day for two minutes each time, that's twelve minutes a day, or eighty-four minutes a week. Spread that over a sixty-year period, and you're on your feet 4,380 hours more than your wife is. No wonder you keel over first. And with all that muscle, you weigh more than her, which takes extra energy. It's probably equivalent to ten thousand extra hours on your feet!

So how do we level the playing field? Well, I don't think it's reasonable or desirable to ask women to stand up, so the obvious solution is to get men to sit down. We'll live longer and we'll live neater and dryer. I know this is a terrible blow to anyone who works in the urinal business, but this is one of those situations where you've got to look at the greater good. I think it's a valid point and I'm asking for your vote. All those in favour, don't stand up.

LAST WORDS OF MEN

- Don't bother holding the ladder, I'll be fine.
- I'm not going to the doctor. I'm sure it's just indigestion.
- I'm not going to let a little snowstorm get in the way of my trip.
- I fixed the brakes myself and saved a bundle.
- Watch this.
- Go ahead, give me your best punch.
- Keep the gas can close by in case the fire starts to die out.
- What does this button do?

- That cop isn't waving at <u>me</u>.
- I'm pretty sure it's not loaded.
- I'm going to get that freezer out of the basement if it kills me.
- So what if the turkey sat out on the counter for a few days? It tasted fine to me.
- That's not poison ivy.
- I don't think the tax department would ever come after a small fish like me.
- I've never operated a 48-inch chainsaw before, but how hard can it be?
- Don't let that little light fool ya, we've got another fifty miles before we're empty.
- You know, Honey, in the last couple of years you've really packed on the beef.

BUSTER'S FIFTIETH ANNIVERSARY

Dear Diary,

Tonight was our fiftieth anniversary. It was a great party and, thanks to an unexpected death, we were able to get the Legion on short notice. It was almost a 100 per cent turnout (see unexpected death above) and I think everybody had a good time.

I can't believe we've been married fifty years. It seems longer. And probably it should have been. Our son got up to the mike and toasted our fiftieth by announcing that he was fifty-one. Everybody laughed, but it was embarrassing to both me and my wife and his older sister. On the other hand, I never really liked him all that much, so it was no big deal.

Some of the guys got up and said a few things I didn't really understand, but I appreciated them being there, probably because I didn't understand what they said. My wife really seemed to enjoy the evening. Guests would ask her what fifty years of marriage is like and she'd get kind of misty-eyed and smile and then do that funny thing where she takes her finger and pretends to slit her throat.

One of the kids had put together a video showing clips from our wedding and family get-togethers and that time when I pretended to be a crossing guard and then their mother bailing me out. The thing that struck me about all of the shots from the family parties was that everybody was smiling, except my father-in-law, but that was probably because he was footing the bill.

But still we had a pretty darn happy family, and as I explained to my wife's father, you get what you pay for. I even got up and said a few words, which I very rarely do, and I think everybody found out why. It's funny how you can think you're saying one thing and it comes out completely different. For example, I know my wife's mother's name is Eloise and I like her fine and I've never ever commented on her weight challenges, so why, out of the blue, I would refer to her as "Hippo" is beyond me.

I don't blame her for not accepting my apology. Which is why I didn't apologize. And it's not because I was drunk. I don't drink like I used to. I sure miss that, but on the other hand, I'm alive, so that's a pretty good trade-off.

So now we're home and as I look back over the last fifty years, if I had known what I was up against, I would never have made it. But I had a lot of help from my wife and the kids and my bosses and the parole officer and all in all, at the end of the day, I would say I'm a very lucky man. Now excuse me while I zip off to bed and see if that trend continues.

BUSTER'S LAST STAND

Buster asked that this be read at his funeral.

Friends and family. I'm writing this now because it will be very difficult to do after I'm dead and I'm not sure where I'd find a pen. I hope this is being read to you by somebody with a loud, clear voice. Moose would be a good choice, but don't let him ad lib.

I've never had a lot of money or personal possessions and I wouldn't know what to do with them anyway, so I'm leaving everything to my wife, Wanda. She'll know what to do. She's always been the decision maker. I know Flinty McClintock has always had his eye on my ATV, but I'm sure if you make Wanda a decent offer, she'd be glad to sell it to you. And it would be the first time you've made a decent offer to any woman.

Now that we've disposed of my personal possessions, I would like to share a few thoughts I have about life and love and any other mild irritants. I've had good friends and bad friends, but I'd like to thank any of them who stayed the same through the years. Even if they were thieves, as long as they were always thieves, I was fine with it. It's when an honest man becomes a thief that I get confused.

So thank you to those friends who remained loyal and true. To the various bosses I've worked for throughout my life, I appreciated the employment and I'm sure you meant well. To my children, who are no longer juveniles and are by now well into adultery, I tried to let you see every aspect of married life so you could make up your own minds and govern yourselves accordingly. I may not have been the best father, but I was there every day and in time I hope you see that as a positive.

And finally, to my wife, Wanda, I'd like to thank you for giving me such a good life. I know we had our ups and downs and I'm sure neither Heaven nor Hell has anything to show me that I haven't seen before, but all in all it's been a great ride. I can think of many happy times throughout our married life. All the times when I was frightened but couldn't show it. All the times when I was hammered but couldn't hide it.

So thank you, Wanda. I don't mind dying, because I had a good life and I don't feel cheated and that's because of you. If, after I'm dead, I'm only allowed to miss one thing, I will miss you.

In conclusion, let me just say to all of you that life is good. And if you believe that, it will be. But when all is said and done, I've said it all and now I'm done. I enjoyed the carnival, but it's over and it's time for me to lie down. If there is such a thing as reincarnation, that would be nice, but I hope it doesn't happen right away.

THE GIFT THAT KEEPS ON GIVING

If you've done everything correctly, or at least enough things correctly, and you've had your share of good luck, you may eventually get to the point where you realize that you absolutely married the right woman. You'll feel a wave of affection and immense gratitude and you'll have the urge to let her know how you feel. I know you've spent many years controlling and perhaps even medicating your urges, but this is one you really need to carry through on. You've got to let her know just how deep and profound your love for her has grown to be. Here's how to do it.

- Stop at the florist's shop and buy the biggest bunch of flowers you can find. They don't have to be the freshest, 'cause they only have to last one night. But it needs to be an impressive display.

- Stop at the wine store and get a bottle of their most expensive local champagne. If you live in Milwaukee, the local champagne might be beer, but hey, put a cork in it. And while you're at it, put a cork in the bottle too.
- Prepare the nicest dinner you can and hide the delivery boxes.
- Have candles lit on the table and the wine breathing when she gets home.
- Have a bubble bath waiting and her satin lounging outfit spread out on the bed. If she doesn't have a satin lounging outfit, use her jogging pants and one of your bowling shirts.
- Offer to wash her back, and take no offence at her response. Then go and wait in the dining room for her arrival.
- When she gets there, hold her chair and resist the temptation to pull it away as she sits down.
- Dim the lights and serve dinner. Ask her about her day and anything else you can think of. Let her lead the conversation.
- Offer chocolate ice cream for dessert, but scrape it off the Fudgsicle stick before serving.
- Pour the wine and offer a toast. Make it a whole-wheat toast. It's healthier.
- Kiss her gently as you reach into your smoking jacket, or just your jacket if it's stopped smoking by now, and pull out a beautifully wrapped gift with a matching bow. Hand it to her with extreme humility.
- It's not her birthday. It's not your anniversary. You're not in trouble. It's just a miracle—a gift to her for no reason other than your affection for her.
- She'll pretend to be so impressed with the gesture that she won't care what's in the box. She's lying.
- She'll unwrap the gift slowly and then carefully open the rich-looking box, unfold the silk paper, and there it

is. Her eyes will widen. Her mouth will open. She won't be able to believe what you've given her: the television remote! The ultimate sign that you surrender your heart, your mind and your life to her. And anything else that she wants, but that's for later.

I know it's a big ask, but if you do it right, it's a decision that you will never regret. And if you do it wrong, you can always buy a replacement remote and wait until her batteries run out.

CONFLICT RESOLUTION FORM
10637420933352098854-B

YOUR NAME: _____

YOUR NICKNAME: _____
(If name not Nick, give alias)

ADDRESS: _____

ADDRESS OF SPOUSE: _____
(If different than your address, estimate how long before she comes back)

____ DAYS ____ WEEKS ____ MONTHS ____ YEARS ____ DECADES

DOES IT BOTHER YOU THAT THIS DOCUMENT IS NOT IN FRENCH?

____ OUI ____ NON ____ JE NE SAIS PAS

I.   WHAT INITIALLY CAUSED THE MISUNDERSTANDING?
     (CHECK ONE)
____ SOMETHING YOU SAID
____ SOMETHING YOU DID
____ SOMETHING YOU DIDN'T SAY
____ SOMETHING YOU DIDN'T DO
____ NONE OF THE ABOVE

(If you answered "none of the above," repeat the question. If necessary, consult with your wife. Or the neighbours. Or the police.)

2.   HOW WOULD YOU DESCRIBE YOUR WIFE'S REACTION TO YOUR TRANSGRESSION?
____ CALM
____ NOT CALM
____ AGITATED
____ HOMICIDAL

3.   HOW DID YOU HANDLE YOUR WIFE'S ANGER?
____ YELLED BACK
____ WENT OUT TO THE GARAGE
____ TOOK OFF MY SHIRT
____ TURNED UP THE TV

4.   WHAT DID YOU DO TO KEEP YOUR WIFE FROM LEAVING?
____ NOTHING
____ HID THE CAR KEYS
____ MADE HER A REALLY BIG HOAGIE
____ STARTED DOING THE LAUNDRY

(If your wife has been gone for more than three days, go to Question 5. If not, wait until next week.)

5.   IN THE TIME SINCE THE ALTERCATION, HOW MUCH HAS YOUR OPINION CHANGED REGARDING WHO'S AT FAULT?
____ A LOT
____ SOMEWHAT
____ NOT NEARLY ENOUGH
(Keep coming back to this question until you answer "A lot")

6. WOULD YOU LIKE TO RESOLVE THIS ISSUE AND HAVE YOUR WIFE MOVE BACK HOME?

____ YEAH

____ HELL YEAH

7. WHAT ARE YOU WILLING TO DO TO GET HER TO COME BACK?

____ BUY HER SOMETHING

____ BE NICE TO HER FOR THE REST OF THE DAY

____ APOLOGIZE

____ APOLOGIZE SINCERELY

8. HOW DO YOU PLAN TO COMMUNICATE YOUR FEELINGS TO HER?

____ EMAIL

____ VOICEMAIL

____ TELL YOUR BUDDY TO TELL HER BROTHER TO TELL HER

____ SHE'LL FIGURE IT OUT

____ TALK TO HER LIVE AND IN PERSON

9. WHAT DO YOU THINK WOULD MAKE HER FORGIVE YOU?

____ LACK OF ALTERNATIVES

____ SHE ALWAYS HAS

____ I'M A MAJOR PRIZE

____ I'M GONNA TREAT HER BETTER

10. LOOKING AT YOUR MARRIAGE AS A PARTNERSHIP, WHAT PERCENTAGE WOULD YOU SAY YOU CONTROL?

____ 50

____ BETWEEN 0 AND 1.5

____ IT VARIES BUT NEVER DROPS BELOW 51

11. WHAT IS THE BIGGEST CHANGE YOU COULD MAKE THAT WOULD LEAD TO A BETTER MARRIAGE?
____ HAVE A LOBOTOMY
____ GIVE UP ON A HAPPY LIFE
____ LET MY WIFE KNOW HOW I FEEL ABOUT HER

12. WHEN WAS THE LAST TIME YOU TOLD YOUR WIFE THAT YOU LOVED HER?
____ WHEN IT WAS TRUE
____ HOW DO YOU MEAN?
____ WHEN I PROPOSED
____ WHEN THE BLUE JAYS WON THE WORLD SERIES

13. HOW MUCH OF YOUR TIME AND ATTENTION DO YOU GIVE YOUR WIFE ON A WEEKLY BASIS?
____ NEVER ENOUGH
____ I SLEEP RIGHT BESIDE HER ALMOST EVERY NIGHT
____ DEPENDS ON HER MOOD
____ I COULD DO MORE

14. WHAT ARE YOU GOING TO DO AFTER COMPLETING THIS FORM?
____ HAVE A BEER
____ HAVE ANOTHER BEER
____ LIE DOWN
____ APOLOGIZE TO MY WIFE
____ LIE DOWN WITH MY WIFE

If you found this form helpful, please notify the Social Services Department of the federal government so that we can renew our grant.